PRAISE FOR *REFUGEE AND HOPE*

"The life story of Fikru Aligaz, my brother both by blood and in the Lord, is more engaging than any Hollywood movie or a fictional novel. It is a true-life story of hardship, adventure, and a journey of faith that, incredibly, all happened in one man's life. What a powerful testimony of how God does indeed work all things for the good, for those who love Him and are called according to His purposes."

—**Dr. Hanfere Aligaz**, Sr. Pastor, International Ethiopian Evangelical Church

"I have always encouraged my father to tell his story, and it is a testament to God's faithfulness to those who trust him to the end. I am very proud of my father for his determination and his Faith in writing this book."

—**Lydia Aligaz**

"Our father always said, 'I promise you that my story will be in a book.' when we were little. Now, words cannot convey the joy of knowing that his true story is finally in a book, and we are so proud of our father's determination to bring such an inspiring journey, and we believe it is worth reading."

—**Sharon & Emmanuel Aligaz**

REFUGEE & HOPE

A True Story

[signature] 9/11/2022

FIKRU ALIGAZ

WESTBOW PRESS
A DIVISION OF THOMAS NELSON
& ZONDERVAN

Copyright © 2022 Fikru Aligaz.

All rights reserved. No part of this book may be used or reproduced by any means, graphic, electronic, or mechanical, including photocopying, recording, taping or by any information storage retrieval system without the written permission of the author except in the case of brief quotations embodied in critical articles and reviews.

This book is a work of non-fiction. Unless otherwise noted, the author and the publisher make no explicit guarantees as to the accuracy of the information contained in this book and in some cases, names of people and places have been altered to protect their privacy.

WestBow Press books may be ordered through booksellers or by contacting:

WestBow Press
A Division of Thomas Nelson & Zondervan
1663 Liberty Drive
Bloomington, IN 47403
www.westbowpress.com
844-714-3454

Because of the dynamic nature of the Internet, any web addresses or links contained in this book may have changed since publication and may no longer be valid. The views expressed in this work are solely those of the author and do not necessarily reflect the views of the publisher, and the publisher hereby disclaims any responsibility for them.

Any people depicted in stock imagery provided by Getty Images are models, and such images are being used for illustrative purposes only.
Certain stock imagery © Getty Images.

Scripture quotations taken from The Holy Bible, New International Version® NIV® Copyright © 1973 1978 1984 2011 by Biblica, Inc. TM. Used by permission. All rights reserved worldwide.

ISBN: 978-1-6642-6379-6 (sc)
ISBN: 978-1-6642-6381-9 (hc)
ISBN: 978-1-6642-6380-2 (e)

Library of Congress Control Number: 2022907216

Print information available on the last page.

WestBow Press rev. date: 07/28/2022

To Martha Aligaz, my partner, the mother of our beautiful children, and the source of my strength during our thirty-nine years of marital bliss. Without your support and encouragement, this book wouldn't have been completed. My love for you will last forever!

CONTENTS

Forewords ix
Acknowledgments xiii
Introduction xv

Chapter 1   Early Years in Ethiopia 1
Chapter 2   Meeting the Love of My Life 13
Chapter 3   Qey Shibir—The Red Terror 20
Chapter 4   Escape 29
Chapter 5   Friendly Faces 35
Chapter 6   En Route 42
Chapter 7   The Life of a Nomad 50
Chapter 8   Freedom and Imprisonment 57
Chapter 9   The City of Tadjoura 65
Chapter 10 The Journey to Djibouti 77
Chapter 11 Dikhil, the Beginning of Hope 84
Chapter 12 Refugee 91
Chapter 13 The Letter 98
Chapter 14 Humanity Lives 105
Chapter 15 Northside, in the Horn of Africa 113
Chapter 16 Hey There, Fikru! 121
Chapter 17 Coming to the United States 134
Chapter 18 Life Continues 150

Epilogue 169
About the Author 171

FOREWORDS

"How precious to me are your thoughts, God! How vast is the sum of them! Were I to count them, they would outnumber the grains of sand when I awake, I am still with you" (Psalm 139 New International Version).

"When he saw the crowds, he had compassion on them, because they were harassed and helpless, like sheep without a shepherd. Then he said to his disciples, 'The harvest is plentiful, but the workers are few. Ask the Lord of the harvest, therefore, to send out workers into his harvest field'" (Matthew 9:36–38 New International Version).

When I hear "Kadafo" Aligaz's life story, I am reminded of two things: God's goodness and evangelism. These two ideas are closely related and dramatically illustrated through Fikru's life. Evangelism is sharing the Good News of God's love, forgiveness, and goodness toward humanity. We live during a period in history similar to the period Jesus described in Matthew 9, where people desperately need to hear this Good News.

When I first met Fikru, he introduced himself as Kadafo Aligaz, a refugee from Ethiopia. It wasn't until I read his book that I discovered that his real name was Fikru, and Kadafo was a name given him to help escape war-torn Ethiopia. It also wasn't until many years after our initial meeting on a Washington, DC, bus that I realized how suspicious he was of me (*and for good reason*). What I have been clear about since I began my friendship with Fikru forty-one years ago was that our relationship was a "God thing!"

Two-thirds of the way through his book, he says, "Starting my life as a refugee truly taught me that every stranger is a walking story. There are unsaid words and tragic events hidden behind straight postures and constant smiles. They harbor brutal secrets. They try to suppress them in the deepest, darkest corners of their mind, so they don't have to relive the painful memories over and over." This is exactly what Jesus saw when He looked at the crowds.

When we first met, little did I know about the tragic events that Fikru had endured less than a year earlier. Likewise, little did he know that our random meeting had been preordained since before time by a God who loved him, protected him, and pursued him throughout his difficult trip from Ethiopia to America.

The particular bus route where we met, I'd only traveled one other time; it was very different from my normal commute. I was carrying my briefcase, and my mind was racing with work I needed to complete. I thought the bus ride would give me a chance to complete some of that work. Then I felt an impression from God, "You should try to witness to that man (Fikru)."

In my mind, I argued with God. "I am too busy and have this work to do. He will think I'm strange for talking to him since we don't know each other." However, God won! I conceded, "OK, Lord, I will try to open a conversation with him, but if he doesn't respond, then I will dig into my briefcase and do my work."

God used my reluctant obedience to change Fikru's and countless other people's lives. Most of the people influenced by Fikru I have never met, but five of them I know very well: Steve, Craig, Tom, Moffett, and Mike. These five guys were in a discipleship group I was leading at the time. They were all fresh out of law school and on the fast track for successful legal careers. You will meet Steve in chapter 17, "Coming to the United States."

When I shared the Good News of salvation in Jesus Christ with Fikru, I sensed he was ready to receive Jesus as his Lord and Savior. Normally, I would have given him an opportunity to pray with me to receive Christ, but I was training Steve, Mike, Moffett, Tom, and Craig how to witness. Steve had somewhat recently committed his life to Jesus Christ, so I asked him and Craig to join us for the lunch at McDonald's when we continued witnessing to Fikru and when I invited him to ask Jesus into his life.

These guys supported Fikru in his attempt to get his then girlfriend, Martha, to America through their connections at the State Department. They all pitched in to help organize Fikru and Martha's wedding. Mike opened the door for the first Ethiopian Evangelical Church to use his church as a place for them to meet. For years, Moffett gave a large year-end gift to the Ethiopian Evangelical Church; his gifts each year were a godsend for this young start-up church.

In the mid-1980s, we moved to Connecticut from Washington, DC, and I lost contact with Fikru. Fifteen to twenty years later, while passing through DC, I mentioned to Tom from that earlier discipleship group that I wondered whatever became of "Kadafo." Tom remembered that his last name was Aligaz and did a search on the internet. The search turned up his brother, Pastor Hanfere, and we reconnected—just in time to be part of the International Ethiopian Evangelical Church's twentieth-year anniversary. Many of those men from that discipleship group joined us (now with wives and children) at that glorious celebration of God's goodness. The celebration was held at their large, beautiful church on the border of Washington, DC, and Silver Spring, Maryland. There was standing room only; our group was honored (in spite of our "reluctant obedience"), and we enjoyed a wonderful Ethiopian meal into the wee hours of the morning.

God is good. People need to hear the Good News. We are blessed to be a part of His plan.

—C.B. Nagel II, Cru-City, Easton, Maryland

Fikru's story is more amazing than I ever knew when we became friends in northern Virginia. Newly arrived in America, he was already self-supporting, driving a taxi in Washington, DC, to earn a living. I had no idea what tremendous endurance, tenacity, resourcefulness, and at the same time faith and trust in God had brought him here. Now I know and stand in awe.

Fikru's hallmark in our friendship and now in this book is gratitude. It was my privilege to help him and his fiancée, Martha, in the early 1980s, but Fikru helped me more than he realizes. We got together each Sunday to go to a fast-growing church in Fairfax, Virginia, called Church of the Apostles Episcopal. While Fikru was hoping for a church where Ethiopian people in America could worship God as followers of Jesus, I was looking for my church home too, inspired partly by his example. Between the time Fikru and Martha were reunited at Dulles Airport and their wedding a few months later, where I served as best man, I was starting to date Diane, who later became my wife. Fikru and Martha were inspirational with the love they shared.

I grew personally by coming to appreciate their longstanding, noble Ethiopian culture and the character each of them formed there growing up. They had a profound effect on my attitude toward refugees, which had a result I've never told them before. In the mid-1980s, when I was senior special assistant to the US attorney general, I learned that refugees from oppressive countries were too often given short shrift by the Justice Department's Immigration and Naturalization Service, which regularly rejected valid asylum claims. With Fikru and his wife and brother Hanfere in mind, together with the oppression refugees had faced in Ethiopia and other countries with civil wars or communist revolutions, I made it a personal priority to persuade Attorney General Ed Meese and his top subordinates to set up a new unit in the Justice Department to give fair consideration to asylum claims by refugees.

Fikru, I'm glad for this special opportunity to express my gratitude. Thank you!

—Stephen H. Gealbach

ACKNOWLEDGMENTS

I am sincerely indebted to several people whose help and encouragement made the writing of this book possible. I may not mention all by name. However, my hearty gratitude goes to you all.

First, my gratitude goes to Martha Aligaz, my virtuous wife, companion of thirty-nine years, and mother of our three beautiful children, for her immense support, advice, and encouragement before, during, and after the completion of this book. Her prize is genuinely more than gold.

My first daughter, Lydia Aligaz, is the real inspiration behind the book, and I am profoundly grateful to her. I am also very thankful to God for my other children, Sharon and Emmanuel Aligaz, for their invaluable contributions to the success of this book. They are a source of joy and satisfaction to us, their parents.

I must mention editor Mike Valentino, who took the responsibility of editing this book. I'm so grateful for the privilege of knowing this great man.

I would also like to thank CB Nagel and Stephen Galebach for guiding me to accept Jesus Christ as my personal Savior. Thank you for being there every step of the way for me. You have both become such a blessing in my life and have helped me to become the person I am today. If I hadn't met both of you, I would have been a completely different person. So, I am forever grateful for the true love and friendship you have shown to Martha and me.

A special thanks to all my pastors, Pastor Dr. Hanfere Aligaz and Apostle Daniel Makonnen, the late Pastor Dr. Assefa Alemu, Pastor Debalkie Yaregal, and Pastor Mike Purkey. I am so grateful for investing in me and others. In addition to being a pastor, you are also a mentor, advocate, teacher, and friend. Thank you for always going beyond your pastoral duties to fulfill each of these roles. Having you in my life has helped me to grow as a Christian and to become a better man. May the Lord continue to bless you and your ministry!

And to all my mentors and counselors who have contributed in various ways in my ministry. Rev. Dr. Tolosa Gudina, Pastor Dr. Tesefa Workeneh, Pastor Seifu Kebede, Pastor Dr. Teame Desta, Pastor Dr. Girma Desalegn. Your counsel, constructive criticisms, prayers, and devotion have proved invaluable in writing this book, and I am so glad to be associated with great hearts and minds like you all.

To all my Bethel family (Bethelians), who have shared part of themselves and their God calling gifts with me, it is too numerous to mention all who have contributed to my being who I am today, and for the success of this book, you deserve my mention. I look forward to continuing our service to the Almighty God. I love you all!

Finally, to the Almighty God, from whom all true wisdom and knowledge flow. The only true God who is our help through all ages, be all glory, honor, and majesty forever. Amen.

INTRODUCTION

I probably would not have chosen to walk on the path my life has taken if I had been allowed to make a choice fifty years earlier. But this book of my life journey, written to inspire hope and bring courage to all, is only possible because I, like most men, was not allowed to choose which path to tread in life but was only given the opportunity of deciding how to walk on the path foisted on me by fate.

Despite my status as a refugee, I refused to allow those who forced me out of a peaceful habitat to destroy my resolve to live. Having escaped several imminent death threats, I literally lifted my hands, and the good God raised me. Like Joseph in the Bible, my adversaries could not kill my dream. Maybe you or someone you know is currently going through a most challenging time; my experiences in this book are meant to offer hope and encouragement.

When I arrived in the United States in September 1980 by divine providence through the refugee resettlement program, I immediately understood God had a hand in all my travails. I quickly surrendered to the Lord Jesus Christ and accepted Him as my personal Lord and Savior. I have come to realize that nothing is truly impossible with God.

Refugee and Hope reminds everyone whose present condition may be bleak and challenging that it is not over until you win. It is said that the darkest part of the night is just before the day breaks. My story is a true tale of good triumphing over evil. That I emerged from the ashes of a refugee to become a prominent music minister in a very competitive environment like the United States should help you, the reader, remain hopeful and determined. If I can come this far in becoming all that God intended me to be, indeed, there is no condition insurmountable. Certainly, there is no failure except in not trying again (Abraham Lincoln).

This book also provides invaluable material for preachers, counselors, and church workers and inspires all of humanity regardless of creed or religion.

This is a story for all seasons, "for we all may not have the opportunity to choose the path of life to walk on, but we all can decide how to walk, as victors or victims."

CHAPTER 1

Early Years in Ethiopia

I come from Ethiopia, a country with one of the richest, most ancient histories in the world. You don't hear many people talking about its highly developed culture and proud heritage though. Growing up there, I lived a normal life, but I never took the time to understand my nation's intriguing past and present.

Ethiopia's title of the "oldest country in the world" is certainly well deserved. Ethiopia is a beautiful country, full of natural wonders and modernized buildings and architecture. One could sense the vibrant essence of the past in every corner of the land by just glancing at the country's streets. There were many towns throughout Ethiopia, and they were alive and busy as people carried on with their routines.

Among some of these intriguing places in Ethiopia, I belonged to Weldiya, a city engraved with nature and that possessed the spirit of the rich Ethiopian culture. I am the first child of Ms. Tsehaynesh Yemer and the fourth child of my father, Geraazemach Aligaz Tefera, who had been married previously.

My father was a Weldiya resident. In fact, he was the mayor of the city. He was a hardworking man with his priorities set straight. What stands out about him is how determined he was and how he never wavered from his goals.

If I were to describe his achievements and past, well, he was a first lieutenant in Ethiopia's Imperial Honor Guard and also a flag bearer.

He was trained in the Belgian military and served from 1931 to 1943. As a unit, the Imperial Honor Guard only participated in the Battle of Maychew, also known as the Battle of Mai Ceu (March 31, 1936), where my father fought the Italians. It was the last major battle waged on the northern front during the Second Italo-Abyssinian War and took place near Maychew (Mai Ceu), Ethiopia, in the modern region of Tigray.

Lieutenant Aligaz Tefera, 1932

Several years later, my dad retired from the military and became a mayor. As mentioned before, Weldiya was my hometown. It is the capital of the Semien Wollo Zone and the *woreda* (district) in northern Ethiopia. It is located to the north of Dessie and the southeast of Lalibela in the Amhara region; this town has an elevation of 2,112 meters above sea level. From what I was told by my father, he was the first mayor of Weldiya.

My father made sure that his morning routine remained simple; being late to work was simply incomprehensible to him. He took great pleasure in being punctual. The first thing he did every morning after waking up was open the curtains hanging by the side of the bed. They were gray, but there was no light to pierce through because the clock had just struck 3:00 a.m. My father was an Orthodox Christian, so he got up early to pray. Most of the family was also devout, to the point we would go to church every Sunday and follow strict Christian rules.

Geraazemach Aligaz Tefera

After washing up a bit, Father prayed for three hours. This was his set routine, and praying was an important part of his day. If there was no light in the house, then he would use a candle to read his Bible. And when he was unwell, he prayed from his bed. Regardless of circumstances, he had to pray no matter what. After completing his prayers, he got up and made his way toward the bathroom. Then, following a ten-to-fifteen-minute shower, he would get ready for the day and leave for his office, where several matters awaited his attention. The roads of the country were in poor condition, beset with pervasive mud and potholes. Moreover, as there were no cars or other comfortable transportation, my father had to ride a mule to his office.

He would of course reach the office at the perfect time; there was no way he would be anything less than competent, as he was the mayor. His assistant would follow him with a couple of files in his hands. I can imagine my father standing in his fixed spot, rubbing his temples to rid himself of the last vestiges of sleep, and watching the man with that familiar frown on his face. "Oh, I had to check these today, right?" he would say—or so I imagine. My father was nothing if not diligent.

Every day was a busy day for my father. It is no surprise, considering he held one of the key posts in the region. He would work attentively all day and only leave the office when dusk was falling.

When I think of my father at work, I imagine him sitting at his heavy wood desk, cluttered with all sorts of official files. I see him flipping through some documents too complicated to make sense of for a nongovernment official. I see his eyes carefully reading every word on every sheet as the cups of tea by his elbow go cold one by one. I see him engrossed, his eyebrows knitted together in concentration. I imagine how he came up with solutions to seemingly impossible problems. That's just the man he was.

I also know how my father met my mother. It was an ordinary day, like any other. He was walking down the street when he saw a man whom he recognized, an older gentleman who was a lawyer, getting off a bus with his children. My father approached the man to say hello.

The elderly man introduced his children to my father. One of them was a beautiful young girl who caught his eye. Her hair hung down to her shoulders, while her skin seemed to glow in the sunlight. She wore a neutral expression on her face and fiddled with her fingers as she looked around.

Father walked away after exchanging friendly greetings with the man and his family. About a week later, my father arranged another meeting with this man, this time in the mayor's office. He told his friend of his interest in his daughter, and an official meeting with the girl was set up. That kind of old-fashioned protocol was the way things were done in those days. The meeting went well, and my father asked her father for her hand in marriage. His proposal was accepted, and she became his wife and eventually my mother.

My father already had three children from his previous marriage. I was my father's fourth child and my mother's first. So I had three siblings older than me who left the nest gradually as they grew older to start their own families and careers.

Ms. Tsehaynesh Yemer

As I think about my mother, I only feel gratefulness. She had me and my sister when she was quite young. It felt like we grew up together, so to speak. I can only think about the amazing memories that I made with my mother. She took such good care of me. When I got sick, she rubbed Vicks on my back and chest; it helped me calm down. But instead of the medicine, a mother's touch was what helped me the most. Her warm hands always reminded me of home, as if I were in a safe place.

I was also a picky eater, which is the worst nightmare for a lot of mothers. So when I got sick, I tended to crave special food like *qategna* and *shiro fitfit*. Both of these belong to the traditional Ethiopian cuisine. Aside from that, I didn't trouble my mother much because I didn't ask for a lot of things. Let's just say that I was low maintenance. The most I would do was ask her for some extra money to watch a movie or hang out with friends. Luckily enough, she gladly handed me the money. Now that I think about it, we didn't belong to an extremely well-off family. She gave away something of hers to satisfy my needs. This kind of sacrificial love is something that I can only see now as I have grown up.

All in all, I enjoyed being with my parents. They showed a lot of interest in my school life and supported me throughout my childhood.

Considering I lived in Ethiopia, if they didn't support my learning, I probably wouldn't have had a chance to get an education. When I think about it now, it was always so sweet of my parents to ask me about how my day at school went; they asked every single day. They genuinely sat down to listen to my childish concerns or interesting events at school. This would include homework, my teachers, and the different activities in which I participated.

However, our lovely days in the town of Weldiya came to an end sooner than anyone had expected. One day, my father suddenly broke the news to the family that we would be moving away. I don't remember much about it, but years later, my mother explained to me in detail precisely what had happened. Father gathered the family around the round table set in the middle of the living room. I was only five years old at that time and paced around the place, knocking anything down that was in my way. Mother kept picking me up to make sure I wouldn't wander off again. I remember she put me in her lap so I wouldn't move.

Ms. Tsehaynesh Yemer

The year was 1966. My mom recalls staring at my father's broad figure in front of me. He sat with his hands clasped before him. "So, I got an offer from His Imperial Majesty Haile Selassie," he announced. He looked away and stared at his palms, as if trying to read the lines there. I remember my mother becoming completely still. I understand why she did that now. There was no way we could defy the king, whose decision was always the final word; after all, he was the head of the country. I bounced in my mother's arms to get her attention, but she ignored me and continued to stare at my father, focusing on his every word.

He continued, "I am appointed as a senator by the king, and we all have to move to Addis Ababa."

There was a note of finality in my father's voice. There was no room for disagreements because the decision had been made. The position he was appointed to would benefit the family financially, so my mother didn't have problems with it either. She agreed with everything. And so, we moved … away from my first home.

At this time, however, our family was going through some turbulence. I remember Mother and Father weren't on good terms with each other. They ended up separating for a while when I was in elementary school, and after their divorce, my father married a woman who became my stepmother. Later, though, my parents got back together when I was in junior high school and remarried. I believe their marriage wasn't perfect; as time passed, cracks appeared in the smooth facade. They still tried to fix it, though tremors rocked the foundation from time to time. Because of this, my childhood years were pretty disrupted.

I wouldn't say I had a bad childhood because, overall, I had positive, affirmative experiences growing up. I had a family, and I had the freedom to make great companions. It was a time when I felt happier than when I became an adult, probably because my life was stable, and the country wasn't plunged into a dangerous crisis yet.

As I grew up, I enrolled in one of the elementary schools in the new town. The school was called Christiona Mission Elementary School. At school, I was the quiet kid but not too shy. I think it was because I was selective with the people I talked to; I tended to think too much about so many things. I only had good conversations with people I considered my close friends, though I was able to make a decent number of friends who played entertaining games with me.

We gathered on the school grounds to play soccer almost every day, and I always eagerly looked forward to it. I tightened my shoelaces and changed into a clean T-shirt to start our daily matches. I loved competing with the other kids, especially if they played better than me, so I used to observe the children around me and their tactics. "Oh, so he passes to this kid often, huh?" or "He dodges better than the others. I need to be careful!" they would say about me.

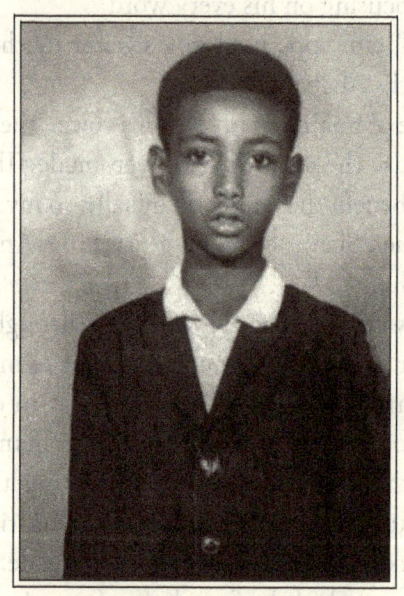

Fikru Aligaz, eight years old

It was fun thinking about the different ways I could improve and get better at the game. The idea of playing with my classmates was exciting to me, even though I did it practically every day. When I think about it now, I realize how I was just a normal kid. I also enjoyed hiking as a leisure activity. School itself was pretty boring for me otherwise, but the extracurricular activities made it bearable. In junior high, I loved the subject of history. My other hobby was participating in debates. Combined, these were interesting subjects that satiated my curiosity and helped me learn a lot about the world and about life.

I had many friends in junior high. Two of my closest pals were Hailu and Dagim, who stuck by me till the middle of high school. It was in middle school that I became interested in the concept of Boy Scouts.

"See those posters by the science classroom?" shouted Hailu one day as we ran in the hallway during break time. He wasn't an exceptionally tall kid; he was as tall as I was. I remember he had a captivating smile. He was a happy, fun-loving person who knew how to appreciate the things around him.

I moved my head in his direction as I stopped in my tracks. "Did you mean these?" I asked with a curious expression, pointing my finger at a flyer stuck to the board. It had the words "Join the Boy Scouts" written in a green and yellow font, accompanied by a picture of a child wearing a dark green uniform. The kid had a little flag in his hand and a delighted expression on his face—no doubt to compel children to fill up the forms and take up those spots.

"I am thinking of joining, to be honest," Hailu said. His eyes were still glued to the colors in front of him.

"I mean … sure, but didn't we say that we would focus on our studies this time?" I answered. I wasn't entirely sold on the idea yet and tried to reason with my friend.

"Oh, come on. You don't have to be that uptight," Hailu prodded. He stretched and yawned and then said, "I'm applying. I don't know about you, but I wouldn't want to go without you." He put his hand on my shoulder, no doubt to convince me to sign up with him.

Ignoring him, I looked here and there, trying to show him that I was distracted and wasn't really listening. Then, deciding to end the suspense, I grinned and relented. "Well, let's go for it. I guess." I threw in a shrug for good measure, to let him know I was only doing it for him and wasn't really interested myself. That wasn't exactly true, however, because I, too, found myself intrigued by the thought of being a Boy Scout.

We made up our minds to visit the teacher whose name was listed on the poster for inquiries. We walked down the hallway and turned the corner until we stood in front of a wooden door. Other children were waiting outside as well, and some even held the poster in their hand. It was clear that they, too, were there to ask about the Boy Scout application.

After what felt like an hour, we finally got the chance to talk to the teacher. He explained to us what being a Boy Scout would mean. Then he asked us a couple of simple questions and accepted us into the team. It was straightforward. Hailu came out of the room with excitement apparent on his face. I was excited, too, but I don't know if I showed it.

That day, I was impatient to get home. Finally, the school day ended, and I hurried home. I wanted to tell my mother the news about signing up as a Boy Scout. It was too exciting for me to contain, and I wanted her to share in my enthusiasm.

I enjoyed spending time with my siblings, especially my older brother, Hanfere Aligaz, whom I always considered a role model. I didn't have a chance to spend enough time with him, however, due to our age difference. Still, he was a person in my life whom I wished to emulate. I wanted to be like him when I reached his age, and despite the age difference between us, I was closer to him than my other siblings. He had gone to the USA to study and become a pilot. When he returned after several years, it was the happiest time for the entire family.

In my family, there were age differences, including a significant stretch between me and my oldest sisters and brother. At the same time, two years separated me from my younger sister. It often felt like we grew up in three different times. This could also be why there wasn't any sibling rivalry between us. All of us remember events and things rather differently from one another. Even if there was an event that all three of us experienced, there were wide disparities in how we remembered things going down.

Regardless, most of my siblings were at the age where they should have gotten married, and they did. I used to visit my second oldest sister, Yeshareg Aligaz's, place to see her children, Yamerot, Tefera, Mimi, and family, as she lived in an extended family. As things were, the tradition of living in extended families was still pretty much alive in Ethiopia.

Fikru, Lackech, and Hanfere Aligaz

I used to easily get along with everyone. This was why I would visit my cousins who lived close to our house; spending the night there was one of my favorite pastimes. Actually, I rarely ever saw my brother, whom I was extremely close with, and I always imagined a big brother who lived in the same house. But I also loved dreaming about a bunch of cousins who had sleepovers with me. Regardless of all of this dreaming, I did have a favorite cousin. The late Fikru Hailselassie was my best buddy for a good amount of time. He shared the same name as me, and we were only nine months apart. I became close to him during my preteen and teenage years. He hung out at my place multiple times. We didn't have phones at that time, so when he came over, there wasn't a way to arrange it ahead of time. He would simply show up and spend the night.

It is difficult to explain, but for me, as the only boy residing in the house, his presence meant a lot. His company was welcomed and long lasting; I never got tired of it. Even if we spent the entire weekend together, it still didn't feel like enough. There was even a time when he slept over at my house for two weeks straight one summer, and then I went to his house and did the same. That was how much we couldn't live without the other's presence.

I think he was a brother to me because he stood by me through thick and thin. I had known him since I was about eight. As we grew up, whenever we met, we talked about our soccer days, staying over at each other's places, him riding my bike down the street … every precious memory.

When I was fourteen, my dad had a severe tooth infection that got so bad that he had to be hospitalized. My older brother, Hanfere Aligaz, was of great help to my dad, as he helped with the expenses of Father's hospital bills. Even when my father was discharged from the hospital, he had to return there after about two months. His physical condition deteriorated further, and we were greatly saddened when soon after he passed away.

In his last words to my brother, Father said, "Son, please be like a father to your brother and little sister," and that is precisely what my brother, Hanfere, did for us. He made sure to grab my hand and remind me that everything would be all right. I started to consider him as a father figure and looked up to him tremendously.

The emotions I felt at that time were a mess because every single wave of sadness and grief hit hard. It was similar to throwing glass at a rigid wall. Eventually, as I grew up, I had to learn how to deal with my grief.

The late Gerazemach Aligaz and cousin Colonel Haile Selassie

I was always very close to my father because he was a loving person. He taught his children to give him a hug and kiss him twice a day. It wouldn't be an exaggeration to say that he was one of the kindest people I have ever known. As a little boy, he taught me that being loving and kind was the most important thing in life. This advice remains deeply rooted in me, as it helped me find happiness and balance in my life. And now I use it to positively bring up my own children. So, his death left a lot of questions in my mind; I was very young when this tragedy occurred.

CHAPTER 2

Meeting the Love of My Life

Like most adolescents, I was naïve, and love seemed like a far-off concept; at the time, my mind was preoccupied with so many other things. However, everyone has to experience love at least once, and my time arrived relatively quickly. I met the love of my life on a slightly chilly evening when I was only fifteen.

I used to sit by the corner of the street called Kela, near Ferensay Legasion, along with my neighborhood friends. That place was always quiet; only the children's laughter rang out, breaking the silence. Under the cloudy sky, we would gather around and play games or chat for as long as we could.

That day, I had just returned from school and was ready to spend my evening like every other day. The navy blue cloth of the uniform was sticking to my back, thanks to the constant sweating from playing outside. I stretched my exhausted limbs.

"Wow, I'm so tired!" I said, my voice cracking. Then I sat down in the middle of the group and looked at the streets. When I put my hands on the dirty concrete stairs, the dust stuck to my sweaty palms. With a disgusted face, I immediately started wiping my palms onto my pants. Luckily, my pants weren't dark, so it didn't leave a mark. In the midst of it all, I noticed a girl pass by right in front of our group. Her hair was beautifully tied up, and her flushed cheeks enhanced the features of her small face.

Her pants were light blue and outlined her graceful, slender legs. I believe I stared at her until she reached the end of the street. One of my neighborhood friends sitting next to me caught sight of my expression and let out a little chuckle. I turned my head in his direction with a rather confused expression and told him, "I thought she looked like one of my relatives." Hearing those words, he burst into laughter.

He leaned back because of the continuous giggles and almost hit his head on the dirty concrete. "Wo ... ha-ha ... hold on," I said as I grabbed his shirt to pull him back up. He steadied himself, and we joked around a bit, but the image of the girl was still painted and firmly imprinted in the back of my brain.

I was certain that she had looked in my direction as well. "I want to talk to her," I whispered to myself, to my surprise. However, to do that, I needed to somehow find a chance where I could talk to her, even if only briefly.

The next day, I roamed around the school to seek out some of her friends. She had passed by me a couple more times the previous day, once with a group of friends. So, I made sure I was able to recognize at least one of them. I hid by the large tree planted in front of the school gate and kept waiting. The humid air was also cold, and I wrapped my arms around myself and hunched my shoulders to keep somewhat warm.

After waiting for about twenty minutes, I caught a glimpse of a student I believed was her friend. I did not hesitate at all and swiftly made my way toward the young girl who stood across from me.

"Excuse me?" I started off with, hoping not to appear too shady. But judging by the girl's expression, I could tell that she had probably seen me before.

"Hey, how's it going?" She greeted me with a polite smile.

I frantically waved my arms to explain the urgency but just couldn't put my thought into words. After a few seconds of collecting my thoughts, I said, "Um, hey! I wanted to ask about that girl that is always next to you."

She raised an eyebrow and averted her gaze. Looking upward, as if she was wondering who I could be talking about, she said, "Oh, you mean Martha?" She snapped her fingers.

As the name echoed in my ears, I finally reasoned that she was in fact talking about the girl I meant. I was sure because I had already heard Martha's name once when she passed by with her friend, but apparently I had forgotten.

"Yeah, I wanted to talk about her," I said. Her stare seemed to pierce through me, but I couldn't back out at this point. "Well, you know ..."

I began. It was difficult to collect my racing thoughts, but I had to put everything into words, no matter what. This was my big chance. "I kind of like her, and I want to talk to her." I stared at the muddy ground, having at last plainly said what I wanted to say.

"Can you arrange something so that I can get to talk to her? Or maybe can you just tell me a bit about her?" I asked. I didn't want to appear desperate, but urgency was dripping from every word that left my mouth.

The girl stepped a bit back and placed her tanned fingers on her face. She thought for a quick second and finally nodded. With a smirk, she told me, "All right, I'll see what we can do." She tapped my tensed shoulder for good measure. If it were possible for a person's face to physically light up, mine would have been beaming at that moment. I left school to meet my friends in the neighborhood, as was my schedule.

My anticipation of meeting Martha intensified. After a week, I finally got to experience one of the best things to ever grace my fifteen years of existence. Once again, I was chatting away with my friends. We had a couple of marbles in our hands and were throwing them around. Our laughter and screams filled up the silence in the gloomy neighborhood. Suddenly, Martha's friend that I had previously spoken to came up to me. Martha stood behind her with a neutral yet welcoming expression on her face.

"Can we sit down beside you guys?" her friend asked as a smile adorned her face.

"O-oh? All right," was all that I could say. I still didn't know how she was able to convince Martha, but I didn't let the little details bother me.

Martha Aligaz, 1975

Martha stood beside me for a while. I could only focus on her because she kept looking at me with such a shy expression on her face. I lowered my head and avoided meeting her gaze. "Hi. What's your name?" she asked politely while looking straight ahead.

"Oh ... I'm Fikru," I replied with determination. I was glad she was able to break the ice somehow because I was blushing crazily, which made it difficult for me to step out of my comfort zone.

"That's a nice name." Martha laughed. "You probably know my name, but it's Martha. Fikru!" she said with a twinkle in her doe eyes.

"I ... uh ..." The nervousness really got to me, as my jaw trembled when I tried to form a sentence.

After a while, I asked her very quietly whether I could go along with her to someplace other than here. She nodded. "Can you accompany me till home then?" Martha inquired with a chuckle.

My hands were trembling, but thankfully I still somehow managed to say, "Sure."

I was nervous throughout the journey to her house. I dragged my feet on the dark and dusty ground. As we kept on walking, I sensed that I didn't feel quite as tense anymore.

We continued on our way, and surprisingly enough, I was able to initiate a decent conversation. We passed by a shop on the side of the road. There were candies, chewing gum, and lollipops on display at the front. I turned my head in her direction and saw that she was admiring the sweets. For some reason, I wanted to buy a couple for her just to see that smile on her face again. "Would you want some?" I asked as I tilted my head toward her.

"Ha-ha, no, it's fine!" she replied with a giggle.

I wasn't convinced, but seeing her face light up made me smile as well. We laughed all the way until I forgot the time. Before I even knew it, we were standing outside her place. The tall black gate was looming over our teenage figures. A sudden chilly breeze came our way, sending shivers down my spine.

"This is it, I guess," I said as I removed my eyes from the gate and looked at her.

I don't know how the sudden bravery rushed into my system, but I squinted at Martha and awkwardly asked, "Can I hug you?"

She froze for a second, probably not knowing how to respond. I felt bad, as if I had made a mistake. Confusion overwhelmed me. But she closed her eyes and replied, "Sure, go ahead."

I wrapped my thin arms around her waist. She hugged me back, quite tightly. After pulling away, I took her hand in mine and kissed her cheek. Her skin felt a bit cold as my lips brushed against her cheek, but nothing could ever express what I felt in those moments.

I bade her farewell and made my way home. My stomach felt knotted. I was so nervous!

"Yes, this is it. You're in love," I muttered to myself. At this time, though filled with anxiety, I was also the happiest I had ever been. Of course, I didn't know that a harsh fate awaited us.

After that interaction, I was not able to meet Martha again for a long while. During that time, winter was near, so as usual, I had to go to town. It took me two months to return. When I did, I continued my relationship with her.

"The protests aren't seeing an end," Martha said, standing next to me by the school gate. The huge eucalyptus tree beside us made the air smell different.

Martha Aligaz, high school

"They'll probably end up closing the school," I muttered under my breath.

My voice sounded disappointed, and Martha noticed that. "I heard that, you know?" she replied with her usual happy tone. She was always so cheerful and caring; there was never a time where it appeared she didn't appreciate my presence.

Much to my dismay, I was right; the school did end up closing because of the ongoing protests and the disruption within the government. Even though it was for our safety, I didn't appreciate it because that meant I couldn't meet Martha anymore.

Martha Aligaz, high school

The country underwent a sudden terrible change. There were protests against the system, while the people in power were killing off anyone who dared to get in their way. In retrospect, I would say this was when my childhood was finally over. I was exposed to violence and bloodshed for the first time, which effectively divested me of the innocent notion that humans were all benign, kind creatures. All that met my eyes during this time was murder and misery, which was everywhere.

This wasn't the Ethiopia I had grown up in. I felt like running away from the terrible reality I saw unfolding around me every day. Things were not the same anymore—not in my personal life and not in the larger world external to my home. I was still a young kid, though, and I had to find ways to cope. So, I became an expert at hiding. I thought if I hid from view, nothing bad would happen to the people I loved the most in the world.

The terrible oppression that gripped Ethiopia during those dark days, known as the Red Terror, spread like wildfire that destroyed entire forests. The government ruthlessly used systemic threats and killings to intimidate its opponents. The violence was not limited to a conflict between the government and the demonstrators but also targeted innocent citizens. More than ten thousand people would eventually lose their lives, crushed by the brutal tactics of the government. A huge storm loomed on the horizon. Darkness slowly enveloped everything. Little did I know that these painful times were just the beginning of a long period of conflict that would completely change the country I loved.

CHAPTER 3

Qey Shibir—The Red Terror

I was a normal child with a life that revolved around the chains of school, and that was for the best. However, living in an underdeveloped country made me long for a better home. If I could remember Ethiopia as a peaceful and loving country during my childhood, it would be an unreal experience because such a memory would be false. I remember seeing bodies left by the side of the road to announce the killing of the night before. Anyone who examined a pile of bodies to see if friends or family were there was subject to execution or imprisonment themselves. Family members were not even allowed to cry. In other cases, relatives had to pay $100 Ethiopian birr for each "bullet" used to return the body. There were also large-scale arrests of suspected EPRP supporters. Many prisoners were tortured, detained for a while, and then many disappeared. My family and I could barely leave our home because of the constant killing outside. It was difficult to step foot outside and not be met with a bullet to the face. How could one protect children from the horrific sight of fresh blood spilled on the streets? What kind of explanation could one even try to offer? The dried-up dark red blood was engraved all over the land and served as a bleak reminder that human life was made to end. The terrible realization that I could be a victim of the exact same fate that so many others met not only sent chills down my spine but also froze up my insides.

Nevertheless, I needed to somehow support the family and had to find work. That was when I had an idea and decided to discuss it with one of my best friends at the time, Hailu, my childhood best friend. I met him somewhere close to my house. We stood by the side of the street, the mud from the uneven roads slathering our shoes. It wasn't a pleasant day; nothing at that time, not even the weather, wanted to cooperate with us. The sunlight felt hot as red coals, burning our scalps as we stood under an open sky. It was so warm that when I placed a hand on the top of my head, I couldn't stand the burning sensation for more than fifteen seconds.

At first, Hailu and I didn't speak much because, at some point, we could understand what the other wanted to say. We were living in a country where people were losing their lives over such small things as their beliefs and ideologies. I knew that the situation was very different abroad, and it would be a lie to say that I didn't wish I had been born in a different land. The pride and hope that we once had for our nation as kids died out amid all of the bloodshed and chaos. It was reduced to a mesh of anger and resentment that we felt for this godforsaken place, which contributed to the continuous misery we woke up to every morning.

"We need to find work," Hailu said. I nodded slightly to signal that I was listening, but my mind had drifted elsewhere.

"Do you know that town called Gewane?" I asked suddenly. I rubbed my clammy hands together and sighed loudly. Then, leaning on the discolored wall behind me, I told him, "We can find a job there."

Hailu replied, "I guess that is right. We can take the risk of going there."

The next day, I informed my mother about my plan and explained that I was going for a good cause. They objected to it quite strongly at first, but then they agreed when I convinced them I'd be safe there. That small town was better for us than the city in which we were now living.

As a couple of weeks passed, Hailu and I packed up our stuff and swiftly made our way toward the town of Gewane. Gewane is a city in northeastern Ethiopia. Located in the Afar region, the distance between Addis Ababa and Gewane is 371 kilometers by road. It was a tiring journey, but the town wasn't too far away. We were youngsters determined enough to cross oceans just so that we could taste an ounce of safety.

I was worried about my family that I had left behind; I didn't want them to experience any sort of harm. It was a difficult move but one I had to make. Journeying on, we reached the town in due time. A government farm was located there, so we knew we could somehow find a job connected to that. We stuffed our necessities into our worn-out bags and finally reached the location.

"I wonder where the owner is," Hailu said as he curiously peeked behind me.

"Yeah, we need to find him," I said. We wandered in the fields for a while and eventually reached the middle of the town, which was the base for most jobs. Suddenly, a man with a grim look on his face passed by us. He appeared well off and different from the workers plowing the field. We looked at each other with surprise, and I decided to ask the man if he had any work for us.

"We came all the way from the city, sir," I started off; there was no time to waste. The man listened to my words seriously, as if he had seen many other people who came to him with the same concern. He was willing to give Hailu and me a chance because, considering the situation of the country, people were desperate.

"We are educated! Is there any opportunity that you can offer us?" I asked. I could feel my voice tremble slightly, as the last words of my sentence came out a bit shaky. Nervousness quickly took over my body, and I sensed my chest tightening. I took a few deep breaths just so I could rid myself of the sudden tension that had gripped me. Regardless, I handled the situation accordingly, and the man took an interest.

He asked us a few other questions and tested our skills. Then he came to the final decision of hiring us as assistant accountants. At first, I felt like I might not be able to adjust well, but after a couple of weeks, I got used to the workload. The workplace was friendly and encouraging.

Though waking up early in the morning every day was a difficult task, it was way better than waking to the crackle of gunfire. Our workplace couldn't provide us with a place to sleep, so they rented us rooms in a hotel. We worked and then stayed at the hotel.

During the afternoon, the weather was the worst. This one time, I sat in my seat, playing with numbers on one of the files. There was a pile of other files next to me that still needed my attention. It was so hot that sweat poured down my forehead. The clock had just struck 2:00 p.m., and the walls of our office had pretty much turned into laser beams. My throat felt incredibly dry while I kept dabbing at my forehead with a piece of cloth. "Oh, man … it's so hot in here," I said.

I let go of the black pen in my hand and sighed as I saw it roll down the desk and fall to the floor.

"I know. It's insanely hot in the afternoons," Hailu replied. He lifted up his arms to show me the sweat rings around his armpits. I let out a little laugh at that, but it didn't divert my mind from the heat.

My breathing became heavy, and my eyelids were droopy from waking up so much earlier than I was accustomed to.

As it was only our second month, it was difficult for me to communicate with everybody else because I just didn't know them well enough. Even if we felt sick, we still had to carry on the work.

"The city's a mess while we're dying from the heat here. That's great, right?" Hailu said sarcastically. I glanced in his direction. He was using a file to fan himself. His cheeks were puffed up; I could even see a hint of redness on his dark skin.

Getting to work every day was not easy. We always took a Land Rover and covered fifty miles. Whenever we got into the vehicle to reach the workplace or our hotel, it was always a shaky ride. Once, I even hit my head on the roof of the car because there was a giant pothole in the road, and the tire dipped right into it.

However, I didn't like to complain because it was a privilege that I was even alive. There were countless other people just like me who wanted to support their families but couldn't do so because their fate never let it happen. This was another reason why I didn't like talking to a lot of people at the workplace, because it was scary; the situation didn't allow me to trust people that easily. I didn't know when the rebels would come and take my friend and me away.

I calculated every risk and looked into every concern throughout my years in Gewane. I worked as an accountant for about one to two years, and during these years, the condition of the country improved. The Qey Shibir had relatively calmed down, but I knew that the killing was still going on, so I remained on edge.

This revolution had not only caused tensions for my family and me but had also contributed to my separation from Martha. We met daily before the Qey Shibir started, and I believed those days to be some of the most fulfilling days of my life.

That entire time was hard on me, but I always remembered her. After about a year, I learned that she was involved in some sports activities, but I still couldn't figure out her whereabouts. It was probably my luck, or maybe fate started to work in our favor, but I got to reconnect with Martha when I finally reached Addis Ababa, where I had gone to take care of some business related to my job. The miracle occurred when I was roving the streets. I needed to go away from Gewane and return to my family in Addis Ababa.

I finally saw Martha again after two years of separation. As I saw Martha standing by the bus station near Lion Zoo (Sidist Kilo), she was carrying a duffel sports bag and wearing a gray athletic suit. The station wasn't crowded, so I could clearly see that it was her. I was standing all the way across from her location, so I jogged over to reach her. I was still able to perfectly recognize her. How could I not? This interaction at long last gave me the opportunity to bridge the distance that had come between us. I was able to rebuild our lost relationship. Despair weighed down my every step. I called her name. I doubled over and put my hands on my knees, trying to catch my breath. When I moved my head up to meet her eyes, I could see a look of horror and shock stabbing her face.

I don't think I had ever seen her display such a look before.

"Hey, it's me!" I said as I extended my arms as a gesture for her to launch herself into my embrace. She immediately grabbed my arms and pulled me close. After hugging it out for fifteen minutes, we chatted for a while, asking each other what we were up to for the past three years, and exchanged phone numbers.

Two days later, we had an appointment to meet near the St. George Church bus station. Martha arrived an hour late, and we started to feel hungry. Naturally, I asked, "Want to grab something to eat? I know a great restaurant around here!"

Fikru Aligaz before leaving Ethiopia

She went with my suggestion, and we took the taxi to the restaurant. It was dinnertime, so the place was bustling, but we luckily got a table for two. Sitting by the window, I was able to look at the bystanders while enjoying the view. However, there was nothing there for me to enjoy because I had already decided that I was going to leave my country. Martha was scanning the menu with curiosity. She kept reading the different ingredients that were involved in making the dishes. We contemplated our choices for a moment and then decided to order several items of food; coincidentally, both of us hadn't eaten anything since morning.

We filled our stomachs with a variety of meat, vegetables, and traditional spices. The entire time, a single thought loomed over my head. How was I supposed to tell Martha that I was thinking of leaving for America? I was contemplating fleeing there as a refugee and had made solid plans to exit Ethiopia for good. However, going as a refugee had its own complications because there was no guarantee that I would even make it to America. I needed to tell her all of this but not the exact details.

We left the restaurant and moved around the city for a bit. I tried to find the perfect opportunity to tell her about my intentions regarding

America. I began talking as we sat on the park bench on our way from lunch.

"Look at the birds dancing," said Martha with a laugh. Her eyes were glued to the sunset that was painting the sky in so many colors. I cleared my throat to catch her attention, but she was still focused on the natural scenery.

"Martha?" I said.

She looked at me and gave a little smile. "Yeah, what?"

I stared deep into her dark brown eyes that looked like chocolate diamonds. "There's something that I wanted to talk about," I began with confidence.

I felt her smile turn into confusion.

"I'm going to America on scholarship ... but there is an easy way out for this!" I clarified in the very first sentence. I didn't want her somehow assuming that I was fleeing to a neighboring country as a refugee. "First, I would need to go to Dire Dawa, Ethiopia to meet my sponsors. I'll need to take a train to reach that city. And from there, I will be meeting American sponsors that live there, and we will be flying back to Addis Ababa and depart the next morning to the US." I explained as clearly as I could. She listened to every word I said with the same intensity on her face. In the end, she decided not to question me; she trusted me. We sat on those benches with silence hugging us.

Then I suggested Ras Hotel that had a club close to our location, so we went there. She called up a friend of hers, and we spent the entire night in that hotel. It was a normal, in-house club. They served delicious and light snacks, so we didn't need to leave for any other place. It was built inside a hotel, so we found a room to stay in as well. Martha and I, along with Martha's friend, were in the same room. However, all I could think of was my impending trip to America. I already had talked to my family about my plans and had strictly made up my mind that I was going to move away from them. But I needed Martha by my side. I wanted to bring her along with me, at least for half of the journey. Yet, sadly, Martha told me that she barely ever left her house, so if she went along with me, her family would be worried. My head was empty, yet I needed to think of something quickly.

I looked at Martha's friend, who sat by the corner of the bed with a soft drink in her hand. "Can Martha come along with me to Gewane for a day? I need her beside me before I leave my workplace for good." My breathing became uneasy as I asked the question. I also frantically looked at Martha, who stood motionless in her place.

"I'll go," replied Martha with a determined look.

"But, Martha, your parents ..." her friend began.

"I know. I'll handle it somehow," Martha told her, abruptly putting an end to the conversation. I felt grateful that she was willing to take such a risk for me.

The next day, we packed up a bit and initiated our journey by train to Awash en route to the city of Gewane. Just as we were halfway, I told her that we were going to take a bus to get to Gewane, and when we got to our destination, there was no system of housing, so we had to stay in a hotel. We weren't that hungry because we'd already eaten, but we needed to change our clothes. We arrived at the hotel, and all we could do was take out a fresh pair of clothes and get changed.

After tidying up, we stayed in our room for a bit but eventually left to grab some food. As we got back, there came a horrific realization. Martha's cousin worked with me in the same department, but I didn't know that he was related to her until then. He came up to our seats with a concerned expression, his eyes fixated on Martha.

"What are you doing here?" her cousin asked loudly; in fact, he was practically screaming. "Does your mother know about this, Martha?" he asked in disbelief.

Martha seemed to be at a loss for words. She tried to speak but couldn't. Her parents didn't know that Martha was with me, but I somehow had to lie for the sake of the situation. I said, "Her mother knows."

At that point, I started to sweat, but I tried my best to conceal my anxiety. Thankfully, the cousin left us alone. I realized that it was time to bring Martha back home. The next day, I dropped her off at Awash train station and returned home to Addis Ababa. I also learned that her parents were searching for her and that her mother was extremely worried. I felt bad and decided to buy a couple of gifts for her mother. Perhaps that was my way of making it up to her.

"I don't know your mother, but I heard that she was very anxious because of me. Do give this to her for me," I said as I handed two boxes wrapped in light purple gift wrapping. A bright red bow adorned the top of the boxes. Then I gave Martha her gifts.

"I'll miss you," she said as her gentle eyes welled up with tears.

I had reunited with Martha for such a brief period, and now she was slipping away from my grasp again. However, I had made up my mind that I would help Martha and my family by leaving the country I loved so dearly. It was dangerous for any of us to keep living there, considering the highly turbulent situation. Before leaving, I entrusted my secret to a friend of mine. I asked him not to mention the real reason I was leaving Ethiopia. I lied to Martha by telling her that I was going to the United States as a student, but I was ready to become a refugee in Djibouti. Martha's tear-filled eyes and shaking voice as she bade me farewell were planted deep in my memory as I headed out on a long and strenuous journey. At the age of just nineteen, my adventure as a refugee was yet to begin. I was still unsure about whether it would bring me eternal happiness or a new chain of regrets. All I knew was that I was willing to take the jump.

CHAPTER 4

Escape

I left Martha behind with a heavy heart, but there was no room for uncertainty at this point. I tried not to be overcome by thoughts of Martha and my family. I was determined to pass through whatever circumstances befell me, and I knew that I really wanted to leave this country.

To start my journey out of my homeland, I left my town and traveled to Dubti, a sparsely populated town in northeast Ethiopia, located in the Afar region. The distance from Dubti to Addis Ababa is 394 kilometers. I was on my way to meet a couple of locals, Afar merchants who promised me that they'd help me with my escape. They wanted to leave the country as well, so I learned that Afar's spoken language in the hope of better communication. You might think that learning a new language is an amazing feat, but it was the least I could do, considering I wanted to flee from the violence of the revolution in the country and make my home elsewhere.

I left Gewane at six in the morning, with only some tea in my belly, and after two hours of driving, I finally reached Dubti. There was never a time when this town didn't turn into a ball of flames. The intense heatwave in the middle of the day made me grunt and sigh. Every footstep felt heavy, as if my feet were made of lead. As I walked on, I raised my face to the sun. I cursed under my breath, hoping for the intensity of the scorching rays to let up. It was chilly in the morning, so the broiling heat was a lot to handle so suddenly.

I agreed to meet my buddies at a specific location, so my strenuous journey was to get to that spot. It took me less than fifteen minutes, and I arrived at the appointed place. My forehead was sweaty, while my clean white shirt stuck to my back. My cheeks were red, and I leaned against the wall to catch my breath for a bit. There was no one at the spot yet, and I wanted to scold myself for making it there too quickly before anybody else. But there wasn't much time to dwell on that.

Resting my hand on the grimy wall, I stared into the distance. Sniffling, I realized that my eyes were watering up. I knew for a fact that I was setting out on a treacherous journey. However, standing there and seeing the scene in front of me was a hundred times worse than any of my doubtful thoughts. Martha's face appeared in my head. I closed my eyes and let out a heavy sigh. Suddenly, a breeze stirred briefly, flushing out the warmth from my body. I still remember the chilliness of the quick wind.

After that, I removed my hand from the wall and stood straight. I crossed my arms and glued my eyes to the street in front of me, waiting for my friends.

A minute or so passed, and then Yohannes, a family friend of mine, emerged from the corner of the street. He waved at me from a distance, a big smile on his face, and I did the same. It was dangerous to be meeting like this in the middle of the town. Just recently, two people had been injured during the protests. I could only imagine the violent, chaotic scene that had taken place there, and just thinking about it made me nauseated. I felt like a mole whose only purpose in this world was to hide just to protect itself. I was sick and tired of this life. That's why I stood with my arms crossed, to really savor the determination that I felt deep inside of me.

My thoughts were abruptly broken when Habib reached me and shook my hand.

"Hey, you're here early," he said as he too leaned against the wall.

I nodded and chuckled. "I guess. The destination is kind of far away, right?" I asked curiously. "I think you told me before," I added, and quietly fixed my gaze on him to receive an answer.

"Yeah, you're right. It's a doable distance," he said and dusted off his clothes. He was wearing a plain beige shirt paired with dark blue pants.

The pants looked almost faded because of the mud stains and dust that covered them.

"Seeing you like this really reminds me that we're in the middle of a war," I said.

Hearing that, he looked down at his clothes and gave out a hearty laugh. "Well, putting your life on the line to leave this country doesn't remind you of it?" he said with a cheeky grin.

I jokingly put my hands up to show that he wasn't wrong. We kept up with our silly banter until we saw some of our other companions making their way toward us.

I greeted them, and we got straight to the details of our plan. It took us a day, but we planned the escape. We decided to get on a bus and grab most of our necessities. We specifically agreed to not bring any extra material, as that would just be added weight. As our journey was going to be difficult, it was for the best that we had as little baggage as possible.

I packed two sets of clothes and everyday toiletries. We also made sure to carry small bags so we wouldn't appear suspicious. They wouldn't let us in if we were carrying a huge load. Even though I make it sound simple, the plan was quite difficult to set up. It took us months to prepare ourselves, ensuring that we had covered all the loopholes. We had to arrange the mode of transportation as well and had to gather other external support.

In April, we set our plan into motion.

On a spring day, as the wind picked up and the earth smelled like rain, we made our way to Asayita. The roads were rough and uneven, as usual. All of us loaded our stuff in the back of the bus. Throughout the bumpy ride, I glanced at the scenery outside my window. People were walking their mules, and women with baskets of vegetables on their heads roamed the fields. I could feel my nostrils clog up because of the dense smog outside.

I was living in these conditions? I asked myself. I had grown so accustomed to the toxicity in the air that I couldn't picture an environment that wasn't polluted.

I rested my head on the firm glass of the window and just stared at my reflection. I had to make it out of there. I felt sorry for the people who had to continue with their lives in this country. They knew they were going to die there, just like me, but they had no choice. A lot of the people were poor and needy, and many didn't dare to defy the government. I was lucky enough to build some sort of support that could help me plan out an escape.

So, even if they were buried in this town, I wanted to make sure that I saved myself for them as well. I knew that I didn't have the power to protect my surroundings, so all I could do was hope or wish that things turned out well for them too. I wasn't in a position to be worrying about others, as I was literally on my way to a country that was oceans away. Still, I didn't want to lose the feeling of compassion; I believed that in an era where humanity was seeing a downfall, on the whole, I needed to somehow retain that which makes us human.

It took us more than an hour, but we finally arrived at the town. We got out of the bus and grabbed our bags. Ali looked around and said, "Well, we need to rest. Right?" He tapped my shoulder and gave me an encouraging nod.

"Yeah, we should rest," I agreed. We were able to find some rooms. After a restful night, I woke up the next day to bad news.

"Fikru!" Habib called out to me from the other room. I joined him and sat down. "Some of the buddies have told us that going to Djibouti is impossible right now. The government is taking strict action," he informed me.

I closed my eyes and shook my head. *I knew this was going to happen!* I bit my lip in frustration, staring at the ground and feeling helpless.

"They aren't allowing anyone to leave or escape. It's just a death wish at this point," Ali explained. His eyes looked concerned, but his tone was stable.

I looked at him for a few moments and said, "So, what are we going to do now?"

He scratched his head and said, "We should keep it at a low for now."

"What? No—" I began, but he suddenly got up.

"Come on now. It's difficult. You don't want to get killed now, do you? You should change your mind." He gave me a side eye; a friendly smile was still plastered on his face. I couldn't utter a word because I knew that even if he was smiling, he was disappointed as well.

Later, I went outside to talk to the other members, and they gave me all the details. I figured out that the government was stopping people at the checkpoints. Anyone who the government officials found suspicious was immediately killed. And who was I kidding? That was so obvious anyway. Considering it was because of the government that I had to plan out this unexplainable journey, how could I even expect something decent from them?

My head felt like it could explode any second as I started to consider the different ways we could get out of the country alive. Instead of warping my sanity by thinking of the unknown, I went back to my room.

The wind had picked up, so the curtains by the side of the bed were fluttering. I lay down and closed my eyes. I enjoyed the sudden darkness that engulfed me as I shut myself out from the world. However, the faint figure of Martha took shape in my head. I jolted up. My breath was uneven, so I grabbed my chest, wrinkling my shirt in the process. A jolt of regret hit me. *I should not be giving up so early, not yet. Besides, even if I kept on with my life here, I would get killed eventually anyway. Not right now but probably in the coming two, three, or even fifteen years.* There was no guarantee.

So, if I was going to end up dying so soon anyway, I'd rather take the risk of aspiring for the greater good. I moved to the side and dangled my legs. Eventually, I got up and put on my shoes. The way that my mind was working at that moment, I didn't think I could catch a wink of sleep. I strolled across the room, my head filled with thoughts of Martha and my family. I could feel my temples throbbing from the constant stress I was experiencing. It was as if someone was tightening a rubber band around my throat and cutting off my breath.

I was unable to speak, as I felt I might cry any second. "So, this is the end of the journey? This is really it?" I whispered to myself and clasped my hands together. I sat silently in the middle of the room and prayed to God. If I was unable to guide myself, then I wanted His divine hand to do so for me. All in all, my father was religious, so I also wanted to make sure that I had a connection with God.

I didn't want tears. I felt like the moment tears fell down my face, it would mean I had given up. And that was the last thing I desired at the moment. It was horrible thinking about how I had seen a red stop sign in the very first part of my journey. My quest ended before it could even begin, and I felt ashamed for some reason. If I returned to my town, I was only going to be met with a bullet to the head. I could almost sense the heavy lead projectile slamming into my skull and piercing my brain. The thought sent chills down my spine. I shivered and grabbed my head.

Suddenly, a breeze hit me, soothing my tensed nerves. I looked up to see that the white curtains were flying in the wind. It was getting a bit dark, and I glimpsed hints of the moon. It was playing hide-and-seek with a thick sheet of clouds. I gazed at it and felt a bit of relief. Sanity immediately grasped me. This was no time for me to be wearing myself out like that! I wiped my eyes and moved toward the window. Staring at the scenery for a while, I decided to go out for a walk, without a clue that this walk would change my fate in the best way imaginable.

CHAPTER 5

Friendly Faces

After collecting my thoughts, I stepped outside to catch my breath. I had let my erratic thoughts overwhelm me and cloud my common sense. Each and every thought felt like it weighed a ton. I wanted to rid myself of the piercing pain in my head that gripped me like a bear trap.

I roamed the streets in hopes that I could put my mind at ease. The outside didn't smell great though. It was as always, dirt mixed with God knows what type of pollution. The birds had gone back to their nests, so it was silent. I could hear the heaviness of my every footstep as I walked along the mud path, my head hung low. I wondered how I could possibly get past the government. How would I cheat the system altogether?

I continued down the same path for fifteen minutes until I passed a man. I stopped in my tracks, trying to register whether or not I had seen him before. I turned around and saw that his figure really did look familiar. "Excuse me?" I said, deciding to call him out of the blue. It was only the two of us on the street, so he understood that I was calling out to him.

He stopped to look behind him. Once I saw his face, I realized that I truly did know this man. It was Muhammad! He was a guy I had met at the club at the Ras Hotel, when I hung out with Martha and her friend. He was the friendly guy I chatted with for a while. I remembered his name because I enjoyed his company, and it wasn't very long ago.

Muhammad looked confused at first. He tilted his head to focus on my face better. Then he squinted and made his way toward me. Suddenly, he gasped and pointed his finger at me. "Oh, I know you! You're Fikru, right? What a coincidence!" he said with a smile.

I was so glad that he was able to recognize me. It really did tamp down the negative thoughts that had been swallowing me whole just a moment before. But was it really a coincidence? Or was it the guiding hand of God that had brought us together? He peeked around me and said, "Wait. Are you alone? And first of all, what are you even doing here?" He gave me a confused look. He knew that I wasn't a resident of this place. I had told him about my hometown when I first met him. We had even discussed that we would hang out there together.

I went silent. Should I inform him about my escape? I scratched and tilted my head. *Whatever*, I thought. I pulled him to the side. The street had gotten a bit crowded, and I feared an outsider might hear of my plans.

"I'm actually planning my escape from this country," I said hesitantly, and then ended up spilling the beans. I had a serious expression on my face as I completed my sentence because, obviously, it was a huge concern for me.

Seeing me dead serious as I held his gaze, he understood that I wasn't joking. "What?" he uttered, grabbing me by the shoulders and shaking me. I tried to avoid meeting his eyes because I didn't want to explain myself or give more details about my decision. "That's just dangerous. Are you serious?" Muhammad asked me, letting go of my shoulders.

"Yes," I said. "I guess I'm pretty serious about it. There's nothing else in my mind right now."

He noticed how I was obsessively stuck on the notion of leaving and nodded. "All right, I'll help you with all of this, but for that, you need to come with me to my house," he finally said. Why was he willing to help me out? I didn't know; all I knew was I had nothing to lose at this point. Most of the plan was collapsing anyway, and I instinctively knew I should use any support I could find.

I went along with him to his house, where he mentioned that his mother could help me as well. Muhammad was convinced that this wasn't a decision I should commit to without strong external support.

"So, you knew that the government was going to kill you, but you still just cannot let go of your plan?" Muhammad said.

"Shush, don't say it so loudly!" I snapped as I patted him on the back. "Oh … sorry," he said.

By now, we were on our way to find a mode of transport. On the way, I explained to him how I promised my girlfriend that I would help her live a fulfilled life in America. He was a good listener, so he let me finish before contributing his two cents. I was able release a lot of things from my system. I felt refreshed. But the plan was still looming ominously around my head. Every time I caught myself slipping into a good mood, I pulled myself back to the serious reality, even though I knew such thinking was toxic.

I didn't have the time to waste on anything other than escaping this country. I needed to stay laser focused, and I certainly didn't want to take the issue lightly. My life was on the line from both perspectives: refugee and citizen. Both options were death traps, and at that point, I felt like I was nothing but a curious mouse.

His house was twenty-five kilometers from where I had met him. It took us hours to reach his house, but I didn't feel tired for some reason. The weather was better than before, and the country's condition had improved a little.

We reached his place; it was a triangular-shaped house. It had brown walls and three to four windows on each side of the house. It was surrounded by greenery, and I could feel my soul calm down just glancing at my surroundings. We waited for a while until Muhammad's mother came out and greeted us.

"Hello!" I said with a friendly smile.

She returned the greeting and then started to talk to her son in a foreign language, which I was also able to understand.

"Come on in!" she said with urgency as she heard about my situation. I made my way inside the house. It smelled nice and had pictures on the wall. There was a vase of purple and blue flowers resting at the center of the table. I didn't have much time to continue with my curiosity, as I had a crisis at hand. His mother sat down on a nearby chair and again spoke to her son.

"She's saying that I need to find ways to take you there," said Muhammad, looking at me.

"Why are you helping me out?" I asked. I appreciated the help, but

I was still confused about why they were going to such lengths for me; I was practically a stranger.

Muhammad cleared his throat and sighed before he said, "It's because it's obviously dangerous! You won't be able to survive without a disguise."

The word *disguise* struck me. What did he mean by that?

"Disguise?" I asked, my curiosity piqued.

Seeing my confusion, he grabbed a chair and sat next to me. He adjusted his seat and began. "We will be giving you a new name, particularly an Afar Muslim name. It'll help you get an identity."

I didn't look convinced enough, so he added, "I am the head of the farmer's association. I can figure this out better than anyone."

"Oh," I said. This was it. This was the perfect opportunity. I needed a person powerful enough to back me up. I immediately surrendered myself to him because I understood that whatever way he'd help me, he'd get the job done. If you have power in this world, you are able to achieve almost anything. There's nothing that can get in your way or stop you from achieving a prosperous future. I understood now that I had a great advantage at this point.

"OK, so the reason I had to bring you here is that my mother and I will be helping you turn into a Muslim guy," he explained, right before he pulled out a pair of scissors that were hidden behind his back. I looked at them, and then I looked at him. He just shrugged and gave me a comforting smile. "This is necessary. That's the whole disguise, so ..." Muhammad said.

"All right," I said as I stood up. "Now, are you going to trim it here or somewhere else?"

He took me to a small room in the corner of the house. Afterward, he placed a chair in the middle and asked me to sit on it. I complied with his instructions. As I sat down, he asked his mother to fix my hair. Within a few minutes, I felt a tingling sensation on my neck. My hair was stuck around the back of my neck and on my shoulders. I looked down to see my dark locks resting on my palms.

"We're kind of going to shave it all off. OK?" asked Muhammad. I sighed but nodded in agreement. The haircut continued for about half an hour. Muhammad brought a mirror and showed me my reflection. Even though I was the same person with the same features, the aura around me felt so different. It was like I was pretending. Living in a lie. However, that was my life at this stage. There was no point in hiding the fact that I was indeed going to lie my way through to freedom. All of this was just a little trailer. The movie had not even started yet.

After, he gave me some of his clothes. "These will make you look like an Afar," he said as he handed me some baggy off-brown clothes. They felt a bit rough on my skin, as the cloth was thick. Also, the weather was warm, so I started to sweat after I donned the disguise.

"I hope this works out. I don't look like I'm a person used to wearing such clothes," I noted in an embarrassed tone.

Muhammad gave me a smile and quipped, "It's all right. Everybody sweats in baggy clothes."

Then he said, "OK, so most of it is done. You can take a break for now." He went the other way but paused and came back. "I'm preparing some necessary documents. This'll help complete your disguise for sure."

He placed a hand on my shoulder. I remember his hand feeling rough. It felt like a hand that had been through more than it was made to handle. Even if he was the head of the farmer's association, the determination and hard work appeared to be the same as for any common men.

As I felt the thick clothes stick to me, I realized how grateful I was for the fact that he took the time to help me out without asking for anything in return. In a world where killing a person had become easier than helping them, he looked like a saint to me. I wanted to somehow repay him, but considering the way things were for me, I had nothing to give back. But I convinced myself that successfully escaping from my beloved country was the only way I could ever return the favor of his invaluable help.

I glanced to my right to see his mother busy cooking. Even though her back was hunched because of her age, she was unable to move away from the task in front of her. It showed how she had dedicated her life to that house. That reminded me of how I never got to thank the women in my family. They sacrificed their own ambitions just so they could help keep the balance in the family. As I sat there, willing to lay my life out there, I realized the backstory of a lot of things in my life. I still don't know if that was a positive thing or not because it made me more sad than motivated.

I shook my head to disperse the sudden thoughts. Then I lightly slapped both of my cheeks to shake myself awake. *This isn't the time to be sad, you fool,* I thought. I placed both of my palms on my eyes just to block out the light for a while.

Suddenly, I felt a hand on my shoulder. I removed my hands from my eyes and saw Muhammad standing before me.

"Here," he said as he handed me an envelope. I tried to open it, but my new friend and benefactor grabbed my hand and said, "Don't open it yet. It's a letter, and it has information on you. It'll complete your identity."

I nodded diligently and diverted my attention back to the letter. It was tied up in a neat envelope; I saw that it was taped from the front. When I put it close to the light, I could see some letters written on a piece of paper. But I was unable to make sense of the words.

"From now on, your name is Kadafo! You have to engrave it in your system," Muhammad said seriously. "You must never forget it."

I looked into his eyes and immediately understood that this was the most important part of it all. A name makes you who you are. I understood that I had to adjust my personality to conform to that name. I exhaled loudly as I clasped the letter in my hand.

I lifted my head and said, "Got it."

I felt a wave of willpower take over me. Truly, at that moment, I believed my quest for the border had begun.

"Oh, also!" he said. "Before you leave for Djibouti, you'll need a picture. They'll check it," Muhammad said. And just like that, he took a picture of me with my attire and handed it to me along with the letter.

I was ready to go. I also had some of my previous small bag with me; I brought it just in case. Before I left, his mother cooked a delicious meal for us. I stuffed myself as much as I could because the journey that I was going to embark on was nothing but unpredictable.

Would I get to sleep? Eat? Arrive in Djibouti safely? Would I even be able to make it past the government? I ate the food with all of these questions crawling around in my mind like hundreds of tiny worms.

After the meal, I stayed for a while. Then, the next day, I had to go to the border and begin my journey of fooling the government. I bade farewell to Muhammad and his mother.

"Be careful out there!" Muhammad said to me as I stood outside his house.

"Thank you for all of your help," I said, knowing neither my voice nor my words could express the gratitude I felt for all his help. I settled for giving him a friendly hug.

I thanked his mother as well, who responded with a smile and patting my head. "I hope you are safe out there," she said. I took in the kind words of these people who were strangers a little while ago but to whom I now owed my life. Then I turned around and began walking.

Now I was prepared for my departure from the country of my birth, my ancestral homeland. It was still difficult to know whether my disguise would let me pass through the border or not. But I was betting everything that I had, even my life, on this chance. The road before me appeared long, and I already felt tired from the thought of the agony I would witness in just a few hours. However, this was it. If I turned back, I would get killed; if I didn't, I had a 30 percent chance of surviving. For the sake of my family and Martha, I was willing to take that chance any day.

CHAPTER 6

En Route

I left Muhammad's place with optimism cloaking me like a blanket, yet my heavy heart throbbed in my chest, beating like a drum. The evening wind chilled me to my bones. My bloodshot eyes wandered to the strangers passing by. Everyone, it seemed to me, held a secret.

At least once in their lives, a person faces the specter of misery and begs for it to disappear. They seem to howl at the moon for relief. I believe everyone wants a soul mate, someone to share their misery. I needed one badly. I longed for Martha, who would listen to my concerns and reassure me that everything would be fine. However, I was alone. There was no one to fill the hole in my life. Perhaps I needed to call out to God at the moment of desperation, but instead I just focused on my feelings of dread.

Nevertheless, even if I was numb and frightened, I had to play my role and soldier on because, like I said, my life was in danger, regardless of whether I left the country or not. I was determined to hold onto that 30 percent till my last breath.

The road behind me felt as if it were vanishing as I stood by the bus stop. Doubts haunted me, ganging up on me like vultures circling in for a kill. Yet here I was standing outside the city of Elidar, in northeastern Ethiopia, located in the Afar region. Not once did I look back, ready to depart for Djibouti. I did not wish to turn my head and face in a direction that wasn't meant for me. The thick clothes that clung to my skin and a letter in a brown envelope that I clutched in my hand reminded me that there was no turning back now. The path behind me was long gone. There was only one way for me, to move forward.

I was wandering around the busy bus station, nervously waiting for my turn to enter the city. The wind outside felt soft and cold on my skin. Considering the warm morning that I woke up to, I longed for the evening breeze. The orange sky was covered with thin, drifting clouds, and as I stood there and waited, the colors started to fade.

While waiting, I adjusted my scarf that was wrapped loosely around my neck. Muhammad told me that it wasn't exactly a part of the nomad outfit, but it was convincing, or at the very least the most stereotypical way I could portray myself as a nomad. He assured me it would work wonders. So I didn't let go of my scarf no matter what. Another thing I was extremely careful about was the letter. I held it so tightly that I believe the sweat from my clammy palms crumpled it.

With the letter grasped in my palm like a precious jewel, noticing that the crowd had started to subside, I decided to quietly stand in the line that formed in front of the government officials. Never before in my life had I wanted so badly to just blend in with the crowd.

Apparently, the government was pulling people aside and checking their identity, which made sense because at every checkpoint that stretched from city to city, the authorities were present for identity verification. I gulped, then let out a heavy sigh. I realized that I probably looked incredibly nervous, and that could cause me a whole lot of trouble. So, I shook my head and tried to puff up my chest to instead appear confident. One after another, the people showed their IDs, and the government officer nodded, asked a few questions, and let them go if their face matched the ID.

There were also some people who were standing behind the officer, probably the ones who were considered suspicious for one reason or another. The look of terror on their faces made it crystal clear to me that if I ever messed up, I would meet the exact same fate as them, which was rotting in jail.

At first, I was calm because I was still a bit far away, but when I saw only five people in front of me, I started to sweat. The terrified faces of the people shivering behind the officer added fuel to the pressure. All this time, I didn't dare look at the officer's face, as I was too busy obsessing over ways I could seem like nothing but a normal, ordinary nomad. When only a handful of people stood before me, a dreadful realization dawned on me. I recognized the officer! I blinked a couple of times to confirm whether my instincts were correct or tricking me. But the more I looked, the more I noticed that his face indeed resembled a shepherd who used to work for our family.

The situation was simply too much for me to register, so I began to panic. *What if he figures out who I am?* This question immediately challenged my sanity. I started to shiver because, as I was in disguise, that was the last thing I wanted.

My heart was pounding in my chest. It blocked out every noise other than the man in front of me getting his identity checked. "What's your name?" I recalled that the officer was our former security guard back home. After hearing the name and verifying the picture, he nodded and allowed the man to enter the city.

It was my turn, finally.

"Show me your ID," he said in that monotonous voice.

"Here you go," I said as I handed him the letter.

He didn't glance at my face, so I could tell that he probably didn't recognize me, or at least I was hoping it would be true. But just as he glimpsed my picture, his eyes widened, and with a jolt, he lifted his head to study my face. I turned to my left in my nervousness but then focused on him again.

"Um …" He wanted to say something but appeared as if he didn't know whether it would be accurate or not. He saw me dressed in white with my head partially shaved, looking like an average nomad. Considering that he used to work at our place, I understood that he, for good enough reason, was confused.

He had appeared strict earlier, but now he only looked vulnerable and frightened. I saw that he was afraid, which made me even more nervous. He had no problem pulling other citizens aside when they didn't match the requirements, but he felt nervous for me because he knew me. The rampant hypocrisy didn't make me angry at that time, as I was only worried about whether I would make it out alive or not, but now it does irk me. He kept looking at my picture and then at my face. At that point, I was convinced this was the end because even if he didn't want me to rot in jail, he would still adhere to his duty. But suddenly he gave me my papers back and said, "You can go."

I tried to read his facial expressions to figure out why he had let me pass, but I couldn't find anything. He had returned to his previous state, where not even a single emotion could pierce his stoic veil.

I lowered my head and entered the town. Leaving the reunion behind me, I frantically pushed through several people to find a person named Khalifa. Muhammad had told me that he was the man who would help me safely enter Djibouti. Again, I closed my eyes and let out a silent prayer for him because Muhammad supported me consistently, and I didn't have enough words to express my gratitude to him.

Muhammad had also informed me that Khalifa would be standing close to the bus station and would be able to recognize me if I held my letter up in the air. I managed to squeeze out of the crowd and, after finding some space, stood in the middle while lifting the brown envelope.

I had no response for a good fifteen minutes, which was obvious because the place was packed, and I gradually started to feel frustrated. I angrily waved the letter like a madman, but still, no one came over to me. I don't know why I became so impatient. It was probably because I was convinced that time was slipping through my hands like tiny grains of sand. The more tightly I tried to grasp it, the more it pulled away from me. Another reason was that I truly believed that this country was going to turn us into zombies. It wouldn't only chew away at our brains but would leave us infected as well, and I did not want to become a part of such an apocalypse.

As I was left to search for an unseen man, I felt someone tap my shoulder. I turned around to see a man, probably in his mid-thirties, staring at me with a friendly smile. He was wearing khaki pants paired with a clean white shirt. His physique and facial features matched the description that Muhammad had shared with me, so I understood that this was the guy I had to meet.

The tiny bit of suspicion washed away as he introduced himself as Khalifa. "Nice to meet you, sir," I greeted him, feeling like at last I could exhale. He chuckled and placed a hand on my back to urge me to walk forward. We started to walk inside the town. The air was polluted, and the area was small, but there were people everywhere. Women carrying sleeping children on their hip, huts bustling with noise, and men with heavy sacks on their shoulders. One could see activity everywhere. I fixed my gaze on the occurrences around me to get a good idea about the town, but my investigation came to a halt when my new companion started a conversation.

"So, you're thinking of leaving this country. That is a bold but necessary decision, I must say," he said, nodding as if he understood my concern.

"Yes, sir."

"It's just a prison at this point, but that's only metaphorically, you know? If you mess up, you can go to real prison," he said while fiddling with some keys in his hand.

I looked to my side as I contemplated the possible dangers along the way. I was avoiding the thought because I knew it was nothing but a mere distraction. Yes, I was ready to risk it all, and yes, I was going to conform to that mindset till I died. Even if I had second thoughts, I avoided them like the plague, doing my best to push them right out of my consciousness.

We walked on the streets for an hour until he came to a stop. "This is my shop," he said as he walked to the shutters, opening them with the keys he held tightly in his hand. "It must've taken you long. This town isn't too close from where you were, I think," he said and made his way inside. He placed the rusty keys on a side table.

I stepped inside the tiny room and glanced left and right. There were glass closets, full of considerably old items, attached to the walls. A couple of chairs and tables were placed here and there. It looked like an antique shop, as it had a lot of items like old books, toys, small instruments, and cultural clothing.

"Yes, it was far, but I had to come here anyway," I explained, grabbing a nearby chair and sitting on it.

"No need to sit that far. Come here. I'll fix you some food," the man said, his voice sounding cheerful and welcoming.

"All right," I said, making my way toward him and sitting close to the counter. He told me to wait for half an hour or so as he went into a room located near my seat.

After a while, he came back with a large steel tray with colorful dishes. The pleasant aroma of meat and spices spread around me, calming my tense mind. I could feel my mouth water but hid it because it would be embarrassing to show how famished I was to a man I had just met. He placed the tray in front of me with a spoon and fork by the side. I started to dig in. The seasonings and delightful texture of the meat rolled onto my taste buds. The adventure from the bus to this town had truly exhausted me, so the food not only comforted my rumbling stomach but also seemed to pat my soul reassuringly, as if saying, *It'll be all right.*

While I remained absorbed with cleaning the plate in front of me, I heard a sudden burst of noise. Lifting my head, I saw four to five men make their way into the shop. I immediately recognized that they were merchants from their dressing and gestures. They walked around the shop, possibly window-shopping, and chatted in their thick, manly voices.

By this time, the sky had turned dark. The hoot of an owl howling from a distance overlapped with the banter among the merchants. I was already done with my food, so I decided to chat with the men for a while. One of them mentioned the word Djibouti, which gave me a chance to sneak into the conversation. "You all are going to Djibouti too?" I said while making my way toward them.

Hearing a stranger speak to them made them turn their heads in my direction. They stared at one another for a tense minute, until one of them decided to answer my question. "Yes, we'll be going tomorrow," said a young-looking, long-haired merchant, peeking from behind his friend's back. Seeing that they would be leaving tomorrow, my eyes widened. I would be able to leave this town in a day without having to wait more days! The thought gave me goose bumps.

I silently prayed to God as I asked another question, which was more crucial to me than anything else. "Can you take me with you?" Just as the words left my mouth, a wave of apprehension engulfed me. *What if they say no?* I knew that I would be tremendously disappointed.

"Sure, you can come with us," said a merchant who I believed was the oldest among them.

I sighed in relief as I leaned back, almost tripping. "Thank you! You're a lifesaver!" I thanked them with sincere gratitude dripping from my every word.

As we had already started talking, they decided to tell me a lot about their day as well. We chatted about our past jobs, interesting interactions along the way, and how I was going to depart for Djibouti soon.

"You'll have to be careful," the sturdy merchant replied as he chugged down a glass of water. "These fiends won't let anyone leave, even if our blood is stained all over this town." I nodded. He went on about the atrocities of the government and the amount of innocent, terrified people tortured in the prison cells.

I could only agree with the scenarios that he described and the pain that he diligently mentioned because I saw all of it happen right in front of me, and I knew, from the look in his eyes, that he had gone through the same.

"I think this world can be cruel, but we're the ones ultimately responsible for pushing out of the miseries that it carries," I said, feeling my voice gain momentum. "And that is what I am going to achieve."

With that, I said my goodbyes to them, mentioning that I would join them first thing in the morning. I immersed myself in the thought of reaching Djibouti tomorrow, to the point I forgot that I had another team helping me along as well. If I was going with the merchants, then I had to inform Khalifa. As the clock struck 1:00 a.m., Khalifa decided to close the shutters of the shop. With a tired and sleepy face, I stood behind him, watching him lock the shutters from the inside. He turned around and was startled to see me standing so lifelessly.

"Woah, what's wrong, Fikru?" he asked, taking small steps toward the counter.

I walked along with him and said, "Well, I won't be able to go with you, I think. The merchants that came here said they can take me to Djibouti tomorrow. I'd like to reach there as quickly as possible."

Khalifa gave me a hearty smile. "The people from my side that were supposed to take you there aren't here yet, so it'll take them some time to reach this place. If you feel comfortable enough, then you can go with those merchants."

Hearing that, I clasped my hands together in glee. Still, a sudden realization washed over me. I said, "OK. Sorry for the inconvenience or anything." I apologized because even though he had already prepared an escape plan that included me, I now wasn't going along.

Khalifa simply shook his head and put his hand on my shoulder in a way that felt awfully fatherly. "I hope that you're able to make it out of this country safe," he said, his voice ringing with genuine concern.

I felt a bit emotional hearing his warm words. "Thank you," I said. My sincerity made him smile.

"Now, off you go. It's time for kids to sleep," he said and patted my back like he did when we initially met.

I obliged and went off to sleep. My mind was numb with frightful thoughts of an unsure future, but I blocked out the demons, pretending that my journey wasn't suffocating.

The next day, I bade farewell to Khalifa and made my way to the hut where the merchants rested. All of them had woken up, gotten dressed, and were tidying up the dishes. They saw me and once again gave me a warm welcome. Most of them reassured me that I would easily be able to pass through the border if I was with them, and I kept nodding like the naïve little child that I was.

As we started to walk under the piercing hot rays of the sun, wrapped up in thick clothes, I had high hopes for a better future. However, I truly was naïve because I had no clue that my already traumatizing life would be dealt harsher blows the farther I progressed on this backbreaking journey.

CHAPTER 7
The Life of a Nomad

The blazing rays of the unforgiving sun fell on my covered figure. I felt my cheeks redden and my face becoming hot. It felt like a thousand suns were beating down on me. Sighing alongside me were the merchants who slowly made their way toward the checkpoint. It had been hours since we'd left our huts, hoping to reach the city in time. Even though the merchants had reassured me throughout the way, an undeniable fear continuously picked at me. There was no possibility that everything would flow smoothly without a few hiccups along the way.

I put my hand on my chest and closed my eyes to control my anxiety. The tall, looming figures of the men in front of me were comforting, but my shoulders remained tensed and stiff. The anxiety didn't make for a great combination with the scorching heat. I felt like I might literally melt into the cement wall if I leaned against it. A very troubling, dizzy feeling swirled about the inside of my head. I wanted to scream out for some reason. The heavy clothes I wore made things even worse. But the more I thought about the path behind me and how I had left it, the more motivation it pumped into my system.

Suddenly, I saw a group of tribal leaders standing and pacing around. We had arrived at a checkpoint.

Luckily enough for me, I had been able to pass through the previous checkpoint and was somehow convinced that this one would be a piece of cake as well.

We reached the checkpoint and stood still as one of the Afar tribal leaders asked us questions and checked our identities. He greeted the merchants respectfully. "I know most of you are merchants," he said as he threw a quick look at our group. For some reason, I didn't feel his stare rest upon me. It made me anxious, and I began to wonder if he could see it in my eyes.

"What about you though?" the man said as he looked at me. I didn't know what to say, how to respond, or what reaction to display. I became as stiff as a rock and said nothing at all. The man raised his brow at me, and I averted my eyes.

"He's a merchant just like us, sir," one of the tall merchants said, thank God, intervening to break the tension and get me out of the dangerous conversation.

The imposing tribal leader, with his sturdy figure, buff arms, and thick beard, looked right through me with his dark eyes. It felt as if he knew all of my secrets, about my past and even my future. Chills ran through my body. "Yeah, he doesn't look like a merchant," he said.

At this point, I visibly started to sweat. My lungs could not draw in enough oxygen. I had no words to say, nor could I defend myself. The man saw my distress, or maybe I manipulated myself to believe he did, and chuckled.

Thinking that everything had reached its end, I hung my head low and prepared to give up. Suddenly, an Afar man I had never met, seen, or talked to before came in between us. He had broad shoulders, short, curly hair, and round honey-colored eyes.

"Are you Hanfere's brother?" he asked in a cheerful tone, wrapping his arm around my shoulders. I was too stunned to even speak, so I just nodded.

"Oh, so you're his brother, I see. He's not someone to suspect, sir," the guy said, turning to the right to face the officer.

The leader gave him a skeptical look, tilted his head, and then asked, "So you know him?" as the man stood at an eye-to-eye level with the leader, despite being shorter.

"Of course! His brother was a good friend of mine. They are respectable people, sir," he asserted, with confidence dripping from his every word.

The leader contemplated the answer for a bit, raised his brows, and concluded, "Well, if you know him, then take him from here. It isn't safe, as you can already see." The man gave the leader a firm nod and pulled me aside, his hands feeling rough and rigid under my thick disguise.

I could not believe my luck! Actually, it was not luck at all. It was God's providence. When He has a plan, nothing can thwart it, and He will send people into our lives at just the right moment to ensure that His blessing is delivered. This was becoming a recurring circumstance in my life.

The merchants were able to pass through the checkpoint, but I stayed behind. I hadn't become attached to them anyway, so I didn't miss their absence. I was too busy calming my pounding heart. Shaking off the terrifying experience, I asked the guy his name.

"My name is Mustafa. That was a close call," he said and started to walk forward.

"It was. Thank you for saving me back there. My name is Fikru, by the way," I said and hurriedly made my way to him. "The circumstances of the country are dangerous enough, but I'm trying to escape from here."

Hearing that, he stopped in his tracks and grabbed my arm. "This is a bad … bad time to be thinking of such things. These people are crazy. Do you know what would've happened to you if you got caught?" The sudden change in his voice gave me a jolt.

"No, I-I don't know," I stammered.

"They'll take you to the military camp and shoot you in front of everyone," he told me, his eyes turning dark.

"Oh, wow," I said, my voice trembling. My knees felt like rubber, and my jaw quivered. The thought of a cold lead bullet shredding my brain made me shiver in fear. Again, my heartbeat climbed up, and I had to rest inside a nearby shade so I could catch my breath. "This is insane," I said between coughs.

"I know," Mustafa said, making his way toward me and placing a comforting hand on my back.

He helped me calm down and guided me to his shop. It was a relatively medium space with a single fan in the middle and empty chairs lying around the corners. He dusted off a chair, sat on it, and looked me in the eye. I grabbed a chair and sat next to him.

"I have ways you can safely cross the checkpoint. Seeing a passionate, young soul like you, I know I can't convince you to stop with your plan," he said, still maintaining eye contact. Aware of no other method of leaving the country, I decided to hear him out. "More people are coming in two days, and they'll help you cross the military camp," he explained.

I nodded and asked, "Will it be safe?"

He cleared his throat and said, "I think so, yes, if everything goes according to the plan and you disguise yourself well."

The determination and sincerity in his voice reassured me. I was back to being enthusiastic about leaving the country.

The two nights that I spent at Mustafa's place, I tossed and turned, without catching any sleep at all. A lot of conflicting thoughts choked me at midnight, but I simply closed my eyes, shutting out anything that was damaging to my mental peace.

Two days passed in the blink of an eye, and Mustafa's companions returned to the city. They were dressed in nomad clothes—the same thick, heavy white clothes, but the surprising thing for me was the camels that stood beside them.

There were two large camels parading their humps under the sunny weather. Their mouths continuously moved in a circular motion, and their restless legs paced front to back. I hadn't seen a camel so close before, and the first thing I noticed was their long eyelashes, which clouded their eyes. They appeared harmless. After getting to know the nomads who I'd go to the military camp with, we started our journey around one o'clock in the afternoon. The heat was just as unbearable as ever, and as our light footsteps closed the distance between the military camps, I sighed painfully.

We finally arrived at the camp. It was the lunch hour, so there was a lot of noise from people chattering, having their meals, and men laughing. I firmly held the handle attached to the camel beside me. I was sweating so badly that the handle kept slipping from my hands. We walked past busy men in military uniforms who, if they knew that I wasn't a nomad, would've sliced my throat without giving it a second thought.

I took slow steps, with the camels and nomads protecting me from getting exposed. No one looked at me with any suspicion. They glanced at us as if we were harmless strangers trying to reach our final destination. Their eyes were full of curiosity but not mistrust.

I kept track of my heartbeat every minute because I felt my heart almost combusting inside my chest. Looking at the figures ahead of me calmly moving along with the camels, I tried to copy their footsteps so that I wouldn't appear stressed or anxious. Confidently, I moved on, knowing deep down that if they were to discover my identity, they would very likely kill me.

I had these terrifying thoughts so often that I found myself getting used to them. I was adjusting to the circumstances, and I couldn't understand if that was a good thing or not. Did it mean that I was becoming numb to the pain and atrocities? That couldn't be great, could it? But taking a look at the muddy streets and poor people living there without a choice, I understood that sometimes a person needs to accept pain as it comes. It doesn't make us heartless; it is just for our own safety.

Getting a grip, I made it out of the military camp. I was still shocked that they'd let me pass so effortlessly. All this time, I had been planning the perfect plan to get past these bullies, but this time I was able to do so in the blink of an eye. Later on in the journey, I came to know that it was easy for nomads to pass by the camp because they weren't questioned or stopped. Nobody bothered them. I thanked the Lord for helping me meet Mustafa, who had planned my escape as a nomad among nomads, rather than a nomad among merchants. It was indeed as the Bible says in Romans 8:28, "And we know that all things work together for good to those who love God, to those who are called according to His purpose."

After making it out of the camp, we walked for eight hours. My legs were about to give up on me, and, as we were in the middle of the desert, the dust got into my eyes. I wrapped a cloth around my mouth whenever the wind picked up and stuffed sand into my mouth and under my tongue. After half an hour, we were able to find a giant tree located at a corner; we got there quickly to rest the camels and take a much-needed break.

The nomads who came along with me had food and water, while I was empty-handed. As they gave the camels water, my stomach unleashed a pathetic, almost painful grumble. I closed my eyes in embarrassment and decided to sit under the shade of the tree. Even though it was hot, at least I wasn't under harsh sunlight, so I felt peaceful. One by one, the nomads decided to sit as well. They had food wrapped around a white cloth in their hands.

They offered me a bottle of water. My throat was as dry as the desert, so I appreciated the gesture. As I started to drink, I noticed a weird smell and aftertaste in the water. Upon investigating, I found out that the bottle was made from goatskin, which was understandable, as the texture felt slightly hard and thick.

"Would you like some?" one of the nomads said to me, offering me a cup full of piping-hot coffee. I had to be a fool to deny coffee at a time when I felt like all the blood in my veins had been drained.

"Thank you," I said gratefully and grabbed the cup.

"It has been so tiring I can't even feel my legs," said the nomad who offered me the coffee.

"Yes, me too. We have traveled a long distance. If I had to convince myself a year ago to cross the same distance, I would have told myself no," I said.

"Hopefully you will get to cross the border safely then. You seem determined to do so anyway," the man said with a smile. All I could do was slightly chuckle because I was overburdening myself with that concern as well.

The sky was turning dark, and we sat under the stars eating pita bread and drinking water from goatskin containers. For a while, I was able to forget that my risky journey wasn't over yet. But as we fell asleep in the middle of that dark, shady desert, a lot of thoughts ruined my sense of rationality. Staring at the limitless sky overhead, I felt like I was a little speck in this mind-boggling universe, but I also felt that I was a significant part of it. The stars that twinkled before my eyes calmed my soul but made me wonder, *I am sleeping in a desert, and I am with men I don't even properly know yet. How is this safe?*

I hadn't thought about it before, as I was so fixated on the goal of reaching Djibouti. But looking around and seeing unknown men snoring on every side of me made me feel uncomfortable. There was no doubt that they could potentially rob me of what little I had or even kill me. What if a snake popped out of nowhere? We were in the middle of the desert with a giant tree above us and sand stretching for miles and miles; anything could happen. A throbbing sensation commandeered the sides of my forehead, dawning the painful realization that I had started to overthink. Resting under the same sky as those strangers, I stayed awake in hopes that these men wouldn't harm me while trying to settle my worry over the journey that would decide my future forever.

Even though the entire night, I felt like I didn't get any sleep, I remember one of the nomads shaking my shoulders and telling me to wake up. The nomads picked up their stuff. I barely had anything to grab except for the camel, and we continued our journey toward Djibouti. Again, we had to walk for long hours, taking little breaks in between. Thankfully, the wind had picked up, so I wasn't burned alive by the scorching sun. Five hours passed, and with feet ridden with sores, I finally laid eyes upon the flag of Djibouti flying high.

As I saw the green-blue flag wave at me tirelessly under the stiff winds, at last I smiled. I knew I would have laughed if I was alone. For some reason, even if I still harbored anxiety about the unknown, I nevertheless knew that even getting to this point was a miracle in itself. My every step oozed confidence. I wasn't shaking anymore, and my palms weren't sweaty with nervousness either. Fear, curiosity, and hope all mingled together inside of me as I kept my gaze steady on the flag before me. At that time, I did not know how intensely stupid it was for me to wish for something positive in a world full of such intense horror.

CHAPTER 8

Freedom and Imprisonment

Staring at the colorful fabric of Djibouti's flag swaying in the breeze, my heart thumped in my chest. However, it wasn't from nervousness but from excitement. Knowing nothing and with zero expectations, I let the unknown take over. Every step I took on the sand underneath me reminded me that I had worked hard. It was crushing, thinking about the things I had left behind and the fearful situations I had dodged, but now at long last, I was ready—ready for a new journey and better results, hoping and praying for whatever the Lord had in store for me.

We reached the city of Dorra, Djibouti. Dorra is a village in Djibouti in the midnorth of Tadjoura region, and it is about 237 kilometers northwest of Djibouti. The two nomads stood next to me with their beards wrapped up in off-white cloth. Their nonchalant yet probing eyes wandered onto the citizens of Djibouti, who were immersed in their own concerns. I did the same. I threw a glance here and there, trying to get a good feel of the country and attempting to take in whatever it had to offer me.

Entering the city was simple. I mingled with the nomads, hiding my face and hanging my head down low. Both of the nomads walked nonchalantly, without a hint of expression on their faces. They were used to all this traveling and moving in and out of the city. This was definitely what gave them their rightful reputation, as hardly anyone questioned their presence. Taking advantage of that, I successfully set foot in the country.

This time, my heart wasn't pounding hard, nor did I feel light-headed. I was a bit more confident than before. As I had passed through the absolute worst, I was convinced that my disguise was perfect.

Yet the anxiety returned when I got separated from the nomads. Feeling slightly worried again, I paced around, trying to figure out where they went. In my search, I ended up bumping into a man. Regaining my composure, I saw his buff chest in front of me, and I immediately retreated.

The man was wearing an army uniform; the dark green of the outfit hugged his fit body. He gave me a friendly smile while dusting off his clothes.

"You all right? Apologies if I got in your way. There are a lot of people here," he explained.

I shook my head. "It's OK. It is crowded, quite frankly."

Crossing his arms, he asked me a question. "You're a nomad, as I can see. Just arrived here?"

I fiddled with the ends of my long sleeves and answered, "Yes, we just came in. It was a tiring journey."

He nodded as if he understood what it felt like to almost get killed, travel long hours on foot, and sleep in the desert with strangers.

We kept talking about the country and the people. He opened up the conversation and gladly listened to my end as well. I started to think that I could potentially trust this person. Even if he was from the army, I could treat him as a friend. What harm could come from it? Considering the way I'd met strangers who turned into friends and then into strangers again, I needed someone in whom I could confide. And that was what I did, without realizing how grave of a mistake I was making.

I took off my scarf, ruffing my hair in the process. "I'm not a nomad actually," I blurted out while chuckling.

I failed to notice the changing colors on his face. "I'm a refugee," I told him with a sigh. "I came here to save my life."

Just like the oblivious nineteen-year-old I was, I handed him a picture of myself without the disguise. With shock evident from his every move, the man exclaimed, "What?"

The change in his tone made me shudder. *Did I do something wrong?* I thought, and I immediately realized I *had* done something terribly wrong. I had dug a grave for myself!

"You're a refugee? And completely in disguise? Are you a spy?"

My head started to spin. I was dumbstruck that he suspected me of being a spy of all things. No words came out of my mouth. I stood silently, already regretting the silly mistake I had just committed. The nomads were nowhere to be found and prove all of this to be a child's quirky joke. Sweat dribbled from my forehead. The man's soft expression had morphed into a stern one. He grabbed my arm with all his strength. I winced in pain as his hands felt like sharp claws ready to dig through my flesh.

"You'll have to come with me," he ordered.

"Wait, what are you …" I tried to reason with him, but it was too late. He was already dragging me toward a nearby building. My palms started to sweat, and the lump in my throat grew as he shouted something to the guards, all dressed in army uniforms, in his native language. I understood bits and pieces of it. Some of his words meant that I would be going to jail. A jolt of anger and fear ran through me. I tried to resist by slipping away from the man's grip. Pushing him away from me, I used both of my legs and hands to get the job done. But the man didn't budge.

"Stop trying to run away. It's no use!" he barked, keeping his grip firm on me.

"I am not a spy! Why would I be a spy?" I protested. My voice had the same intensity as his, which I could tell caught him off guard.

"Don't talk back to me!" he snapped and dragged me toward the cell with even more force.

I was already inside the building, and the cell that he was going to throw me in appeared to be just a couple of steps away. The prisoners, all barricaded by dark metal bars, stared at the commotion. They had bloodshot eyes and cracked lips, and they seemed to show no hint of life. It scared me. I was going to meet the same fate. And that I did the moment the metal doors clanged shut behind me, ensuring that I saw the world through the cruelty of unbreakable bars.

My legs gave up on me, and I fell to the floor. The cold ground sent chills down my spine, and anxiety rushed through me all over again. As I sat in the dark watching the sky change colors, I thought of how naïve I had been before reaching the city. A flag giving me hope that everything would be all right. I wanted to slap myself for forgetting that I lived in Ethiopia, a country where terrible things happened.

Biting my lip in frustration, I hugged my knees and lay on the floor. It was already night, and nocturnal birds howled in the distance. I closed my eyes for fifteen minutes. Nothing. No sleep or peace. I kept trying until I felt my eyelids tremble. Tears overwhelmed me, and the looming realization of *this is it* clung to me.

The entire night, I tossed and turned and cried till I had no more tears left to shed. I even grabbed the torn blanket that was lying at the side and wrapped myself in it to feel some comfort. But nothing worked. Nothing could make me feel like the person I had been before. I silently prayed to God, knowing that He was there, even in this dark, awful prison.

The next day in that torturous place began without me getting a wink of sleep. I woke up with the blanket stuck to my sweaty skin. My head was throbbing as if a beast was prowling about in there, pounding the inside of my skull with its big, mighty paws. I was so engrossed in my miserable state that I barely noticed it was daytime. The rays of sunlight hit the middle of the cell through the small window high up in the wall. I kept staring at the rays for so long that I saw small specks of dust flying around. I used to do that when I was bored. Now I wasn't bored; I felt dead.

My lips were cracked, and my eyes were probably red, just like the prisoners I'd pitied the day before. Glancing here and there, my gaze rested on the metal bars in front of me. *How dare they stop me! How dare they come in my way!* I thought, feeling a ball of aggression jump around in the pit of my stomach. I tried to get up.

As I returned my gaze to the bars, my fury grew by the minute. Yet I couldn't reach the bars, as my legs became wobbly and unstable. They trembled so badly when I lifted myself that I believed a bone or two was certainly going to snap. Again, hopelessness swayed around me like a light breeze, and I retreated to another corner.

A good twenty minutes passed, and I heard a noise at the end of the door. Curiosity got the best of me, but I was still undetermined and indifferent. There was nothing to look forward to in a small, cramped cell. So I stared in the direction of the noise but didn't move an inch in surprise or interest.

After a while, I noticed a tray hit the room's floor. The guards were trying to give me food. A loaf of pita bread was on the not-so-hygienic tray. Seeing that, I shrugged. "There's no point in giving me food," I said, a bit louder than usual because my body was weak, and so was my voice. I had to strain my vocal cords to get the words out. The guards didn't utter a word. They just stood silently overlooking the pita bread and gave me small glances, as if they were encouraging me to eat the food.

"I'm going to die anyway. Food is not a necessity anymore. I don't need it," I told them. There was no response, nor did they take away the food. They turned and went back to their posts.

A deluding calm surrounded everything again. It was the type of silence where you feel like becoming one with the world, destroying your human identity and reducing yourself to a mere speck in the cosmos. I wished I had superpowers of some sort to melt the iron of the rods or drill a hole in the ground and escape. But all such thoughts were childish and foolish.

My fate screamed that I was a prisoner for life. Amid my tossing and turning on the hard, cold ground, I noticed the gate opening. The noise of the door dragging across the floor echoed in the small confines of the cell. For the first time throughout my time in this jail, I shot up straight. A sudden excitement overwhelmed all the pain in my body.

I stared hard to see the reason for the emergency that compelled them to unlock the door. I could make out a broad figure standing in front of me, a thermos resting in his hand. His long, slender fingers held the door open. He had bags around his black-brown eyes, and he wore a dark blue suit paired with a clean white shirt. He held steady eye contact with me. The way his deep gaze rested on me made me anxious.

I had never seen this man before in my entire life. Why was he suddenly standing before me as if he were the one sent by God to save me? Questions flooded me, but I shook them away and just awaited clarification from his side.

"You don't look OK," he said to me in Amharic. He was speaking in the language of my hometown. I was confused for a second. But then it dawned on me that finding a fellow countryman could help me out of here.

"No, I guess my days in this jail are making me sick," I replied, realizing how important each of my words could be for my safety.

He said, "I just wanted you to know that I was born in Ogaden, Ethiopia, Somali region. I know your country, Ethiopia, as I'm speaking your native language. I need to ask why you are in jail right now."

I lowered my head, not knowing where to begin, so I simply stated, "I don't know. My name's Fikru Aligaz, and I want to save myself from this country. That is honestly all there is to it."

The answer appeared to be convincing enough for him, making him nod two to three times. He continued to ask me if I knew anyone from Djibouti or if I was a spy. I replied with as much precision and truth as I could. There was no reason for me to hold back or refrain from saying what was right. I was already imprisoned in a small place, devoid of human interaction and basic rights. I wanted out.

He listened to everything I had to say as intensely and diligently as he could. It felt great to actually be heard again. At some point, I stopped being cautious with my words and just let the flow guide me. After hearing me out, he concluded, "I'll talk to my boss to settle this."

My eyes widened. I couldn't believe my ears. Even though I never asked the man about his occupation, his well-suited attire gave away a lot of hints. He had the potential to help me.

"Thank you so much!" I almost screamed. Realizing the volume of my voice, I felt my cheeks burn from embarrassment.

"You don't have to worry over it. We think people should get their identities checked and verified before being labeled as spies. They could very well be innocent," he replied, rather reassuringly.

I was right. This man was truly sent by the heavens above to bring me out of this rat hole.

"You'll be interviewed by the French military tomorrow. They'll give you the chance to clarify your innocence," he further informed me. Before leaving, he added, "You should take a shower though." He pointed at my clothes that were covered in dirt and mud from rolling around helplessly in the cell.

"Shower? But how am I …?" I asked, looking down at my messy clothes.

"Help him out," the man said, gesturing to the guards. Once he left, the guards asked me to get up and follow them. I moved past the tired prisoners again. Feeling bad for the fact that I was able to find the opportunity to leave when so many others didn't, I sighed in exhaustion. I was exhausted from noticing the filthy circumstances around me. There was nothing but distress and suffering in that environment. What else could I notice? Misery, tension, and stress accompanied me like a persistent bat on a dark evening.

At this point, I hoped the wind could carry me away like a leaf torn from a mighty tree. My weightless self could float all around without a single worry. I calmed myself by imagining such a conversion. Yet as the ice-cold water from the showerhead hit my humped back, I almost felt like bawling. The dirt and blood from my injuries became one with the water. Lowering my gaze, I saw brown water pooling by my feet. It all reminded me of how disgusting I had become, but it also reminded me that it wasn't my fault.

Absolutely nothing was my fault. Being a suffering citizen of a war-ridden country, I just desired to experience a fraction of peace for myself and my family. I was not going to back away from that decision or regret it. After taking a shower, drying my hair, and wearing the clothes given to me by the guards, I was told to go into a room for the interview.

With hope still tugging at me, I opened the door and was greeted by a couple of men sitting on wooden chairs behind a giant desk. All the men were dressed in military uniforms, with the usual stern look etched on their faces. The atmosphere made me gulp as I took easy steps to sit on the chair placed in the middle.

I introduced myself, and then the questioning began. They took out pictures of various weapons ranging from small pistols to heavy rifles. One by one, they asked whether I could recognize or name each of the weapons. The entire interview was confusing to me because I wasn't knowledgeable about guns or weapons at all.

"I don't know much about weapons, sir," I decided to add. They furrowed their brows, showing me they were dissatisfied with my answer. But there was nothing else for me to say. I truly had no idea about the ins and outs of weaponry. Every picture they put before me looked to be the same. They all seemed to be guns, some bigger than the others.

"I don't even know the basic guns!" I repeated several times during the strenuously long interview.

As the interview drew to an end, I believed it was better to add, "I am not a spy, if that is what you're thinking."

The tension in the room had subsided, so I got the chance to defend myself against the frustrating charge of being a spy. I had to stay as innocent as a mouse in front of these people, but I was fuming with anger. Imprisoning me and compromising my health only served as more hindrance in my journey of leaving this country. At first, I had given up, but the way I had survived jail and countered hopelessness ensured that God was on my side. That alone assured me of victory. And therefore, I was not going to back away, even if death stared me in the face.

"We've analyzed you very well," one of the officers, sitting to the left, said. He was absorbed in the papers before him and didn't even lift his head. Yet I could still feel his intimidating aura pierce right through me like a dagger. Committing to the fact that I wouldn't let anything faze me, I made sure that I didn't let his presence overwhelm me. I sat there, patiently awaiting a response and showing no fear or apprehension.

"You'll have to come with us to Tadjora for further investigation. Leaving this city is necessary to continue on the confirmation process," he said, keeping his stare on me steady.

I had nothing to say, so I remained silent other than uttering an inaudible, "Yes," though I couldn't understand what they meant by further investigation. The mystery behind these words couldn't be resolved, even when I asked them multiple times. They didn't reassure but didn't give me frightening details either. Not knowing the outcome of this interaction made me anxious again, but I balled my hands into fists, unclenched my jaw, and took deep breaths.

They had prepared a jeep for me outside. I didn't have a clue about how far away the city was, but I didn't ask questions, nor did I obsess over the answer. I listened, agreed, and obliged.

Sandwiched between the two officers, I could even smell the minty shampoo that I had used while showering. The evening sky was turning from burning orange to a mysterious purple. It reminded me of my own life as it went from a normal childhood to a sequence of one episode of despair after another. Even though I was still clinging to hope and positive expectations, the unpredictable situation I was stuck in made me chuckle. As the purple faded into a nightmarish black, I shuddered as I thought about the possible outcomes of my adventure toward the unknown.

CHAPTER 9

The City of Tadjoura

The bumpy ride continued for half an hour. It was almost night, and I could feel my eyelids droop. The distant hum of cicadas in the dark filled up the silence. The half-closed windows of the jeep allowed whiffs of humid air to brush past my face. My head was constantly bumping against the roof, leaving a stinging and painful sensation every minute. I had no room for complaining because I was finally out of that miserable place. This ride toward the unknown didn't scare me much, but being locked up for wishing to leave a blood-ridden country did.

As the dark road ahead was only lit by our vehicle's headlights, I couldn't help but fall into the trap of thoughts. Many ideas and conclusions whirled around my mind. It seemed as if they were giving me subtle hints about my next decision. But there was no use focusing on the storm in my head because no matter how much I thought about it, the outcome rested in the hands of the men around me. They stayed suited in their dark and grim outfits, with stern expressions etched on their nonchalant faces. Even lifting my face to meet their eyes felt like a grave mistake. All I could do was lower my head and stare at their pitch-black boots.

I felt pathetic even though I didn't have a reason for it. I was willing to leave a place that did me no good. Isn't that what most people do? And no, I don't mean leaving a country that is torn by war. I believe every situation in life where one isn't gifted with happiness and peace, leaving is the ultimate option. It doesn't make us selfish or arrogant to move forward and forget the negative. It is utterly human to remove the toxicity around us and find our way toward peace.

Whether we're stuck in a one-sided relationship, have to deal with an unappreciative friend, or are at a job that stresses us out, all such situations compel us to contemplate the act of leaving. And that is all right. There is no sin in believing there are better options to consider that promise a brighter future. It would be undeniably foolish to stand in front of the storm, hoping to see it end but also trying to stay safe. The storm will continue to rage on without considering your security. The safest option is to move away because a storm always destroys whatever stands in its way.

Humans are fragile creatures. We cannot face wars on our own. A single human cannot change the outcome of a grand event because, believe it or not, we can be quite powerless despite being the most intelligent species on earth. So, I didn't feel bad about my decision to leave my home country. Just like any other sane and common person, I wanted to ensure a safe and happy future for my family and for myself. If people called me a spy or a traitor, it wasn't my business. Hoping to lead a successful life void of dangers was the only ending I wished to witness.

That was why I patiently cowered in the jeep. I was nervous yet optimistic. I wanted to grab onto the delicate string of hope and make it out of there alive.

About an hour had passed, and we were still stumbling on the patchy and muddy road. I could feel myself drifting into a deep slumber as my head kept tilting to the right. I couldn't catch even a minute's sleep. The vehicle came to an abrupt halt. The jeep stopped so suddenly that it sent a jolt up my spine. Now wide awake, I looked around. I had no clue what to expect because none of the officers had updated me on what would happen once we reached Tadjoura. A wave of anxiety washed over me as the men in the jeep ordered me to get out.

Feeling the uneven ground under my bruised feet, I tried to make sense of my surroundings. It had gotten dark, so I couldn't make out much, but I could tell we were standing in front of a building. It was a grayish structure, neatly decorated with two windows. Nothing about it made me feel at ease. It only contributed to my curiosity and rising anxiety.

Calming my trembling hands, I moved forward. An officer grabbed my wrist to make sure I did nothing funny. Of course, there was nothing I could plan to do in the middle of an unknown city. If I tried, I knew I'd be greeted by a bullet to the head. Plants and an empty road surrounded us, and it would be foolish to run in any direction. Hence, I kept my calm and let the officers guide me as if I were a sheep, and they a vicious predator.

Suddenly, the officer who took ahold of me passed me onto the man standing in front of the mysterious building. I gulped in fear. He was a big, sturdy man with a rough grip. And the suspicious entrance to the building didn't soothe any of my questions.

"Wait, may I ask where we are going?" I asked, unable to hold back my curiosity.

"Oh, you don't know?" he replied and moved his gaze to the officers by the jeep. I didn't turn my head, but I could tell they probably smirked or motioned for the man to move along. So he took me inside the building.

"Where am I going? You can at least answer that," I said, my voice dripping with nervousness.

At first, I was fine and well, but the more distance we crossed, the more I began to sweat. "Can you just …" I tried to reason with the man again, but the clattering noises coming from the sidewalls cut my question. I could also hear distant shouting and groaning of men.

At last, my suspicions came true as I began to see the cells all packed, with metal bars located everywhere.

Once again, the concerned faces of the prisoners glanced at me nervously. It all felt like déjà vu. I was walking the same dreadful walk as when I had been dragged into the prison in the military camp. The rough surface of the ground, the painful moans of the prisoners, and the aggressive hands of the officer—everything came rushing back to me.

"Am I going to jail?" I asked. I quietly understood what was happening to me, so my voice sounded a bit calmer than before. Noticing that, the officer finally responded to my pleas with a nod.

Seeing him nod filled my head with all the agonizing memories of the couple of days I had spent in jail. The way I'd felt hopeless and miserable, I wasn't ready for any of that.

In a minute, the officer threw me into jail again. The door locked behind me, while the keys dangled in the officer's fingers. At first, I stood and stared at the stained wall. Then I collapsed to the ground. This time, there were no blankets or a big enough window to let in the fresh air. All I could see was a small opening at the top. The cell looked lifeless as ever, as if someone had died in there, and their ghost was lurking about.

Staring for long, I almost felt like I could become one with the silence. My shirt was sticking to my body because of the unseasonably warm weather. The heat had been scorching since the morning. But I wasn't able to notice because of the constant anxiety in my system. Now that I was alone in a cell, accompanied by nothing but my own thoughts, my head spun from the warmth. Even if I wanted to sleep, the continuous buzzing of the flies didn't let me close my eyes for a second. I extended my hand toward the gate in hopes that someone could catch my suffering state. But I was met with no response.

The guard was sitting on a chair outside the cell with his head low. It appeared he had fallen asleep. How lucky of him to sleep without worrying about rotting inside a smelly cage! I cursed myself for taking every moment of my life that I spent outside for granted. Yet I had no regrets about the decision I had made to leave Ethiopia.

Strangely enough, after so many hardships and brushes with death, I felt satisfied with my decision. I only wanted the best for myself. It was this world that was twisted enough to deny me a healthy life. I didn't wish to give in to man-made laws or constraining rules. If this country could kill me, I would fight for my right to get out. I wanted to live my life on my own terms, and I was determined that somehow, with God's help, I would make it happen.

Despite being levelheaded about my concern to depart from this country, the time I spent in jail wasn't an easy one. The next day, I woke up after only an hour's sleep. My throat was dry, and my body felt weak. I hadn't had water for two days, and I'd become dehydrated from all the sweating. I needed a new pair of clothes because I was stinking. I hoped they'd slide in some food like before because even if I knew I'd rot in that jail forever, I wanted to ease the turning in my stomach.

I patiently waited for the guard to bring in a tray of food or even a bowl of water but received nothing. Nothing but the empty silence that nudged me onto the cliff of insanity. I lay in the middle of the cell like a dead body. The sound of footsteps echoed. My legs were as stiff as a tree's trunk. The hideous smell of my dried sweat reminded me that I had become caught up in an unbearably unjust reality.

I tried to lean against the wall just so I could support myself and sit straight. With no energy left in my body, I couldn't even push myself to get up. But I mustered up the strength to lift myself. Leaning against the wall, I saw a guard coming back to sit in his assigned seat. I needed to eat something, or else I truly would die.

"Excuse me ... can I get something to eat?" I asked timidly.

The guard fixed his eyes on me. The dark orbs seemed to be staring deep into my shattered soul.

Suddenly, uncomfortable with the way I'd worded my question, I tried again, "Can I get something to drink?"

This time, without an ounce of hesitation, the guard replied, "Don't ask such foolish questions."

The harshness in his tone and the tapping of his thick boots almost made me tear up. Hoping to try another tactic, I tried speaking, but no words came out. My voice was weak and diminished as if it were a whisper in the wind. I almost scared myself with how fragile and broken I had become. Not even able to move a limb, I remained motionless in a single spot the entire day.

At night, I heard men fighting in the cell next to mine. Their manly voices overlapped with their impatient footsteps while they argued. None of their words made sense to me. It all sounded like a murmur, but the intensity of the fight was clear. At some point, I even heard someone fall on the ground with a loud thud. Their argument eventually turned into furious screams.

After a few minutes, the guards came in and straightened them up. Their shouting was replaced with the aggressive scolding of the tired guard. One prisoner even tried to argue and reason things out with the guard but was met with a powerful punch to the face. I couldn't guess what part of the face they hit, but the smacking noise confirmed someone received a solid, no doubt painful blow. After that, the guards came out. And my surroundings became deathly silent again.

I could peek at the tiny stars glistening in the moonlit sky. Oh, how I desired to just break these walls and run into the fields! Swim across the oceans and brush past the heavy bushes to reach the land of dreams and never return. I heaved with frustration while thinking about the perfect conclusion to my tiring journey. I wanted Martha, my parents, siblings, the people I met along the way, just everyone, to live happily. Was I so wrong for that? Did I deserve to rot in a dark, muddy place just for wanting to live happily?

I wasn't even able to witness the beauties Tadjoura hid inside. Only fear, anxiety, and distress defined this city for me. A curious ride had brought me to a terrifying end. All of it was just as simple as that. It reminded me of the movies where they would lock an innocent man up for ridiculous or unfair reasons. And he slowly withered away in jail, leaving no traces of himself behind in the cold and cruel world. Was that my fate too? I simply could not bring myself to believe it.

Finally, my first miserable day in jail ended. I greeted the next morning with zero sleep. Not even a minute of sleep, just me pacing around in the dark with my intrusive thoughts. Hoping to receive even a piece of bread, I sat longingly in front of the cell. My eyes were as big as an owl's and stared ahead at the people who passed by. No one came toward me, nor did anyone care enough to stop in their tracks and glance in my direction. They walked past me as if I were invisible.

I probably looked like an entity that couldn't return to the normal world anymore. I was just a mistake they were unwilling to claim. The piercing silence and the warm weather knocked my senses once again. Lying the entire day lifelessly, I glanced at the opening. The day was ending. I didn't see any stars this time. All I saw was a pitch-black sky. It was so dark that I had to rub my eyes for a second to take in its dusky nature. The sky was void of stars and clouds. It looked as desolate as I did, sitting in a dirty cell devoid of hope.

It was time to go to sleep again. *It would have been better if they had shot me before I made my way inside this place*, I thought. There wasn't anything remotely positive around me. So what was the point of hoping for something or someone to save me? Absolutely none! I quietly closed my eyes, waiting for my miserable life in that cell to begin again. But this time, I didn't wake up to silence or the noise of the guards chatting mindlessly. I saw a prisoner in front of me.

The guy's worn-out face stared at me as his dirty hair swayed in the warm air.

"This is your new cellmate," the man who brought the prisoner announced to me. He spoke in the Afar language, and throughout my venture of disguising myself as a nomad, I had mastered that language. I didn't pay attention to the officer's intimidating aura or the painful sounds of the prisoners all around me. I just looked at the surprised prisoner-mate and the man standing beside him.

After noticing me staring intently like a child, the man asked, "Who's this?"

With sudden confidence in my eyes, I knew what I had to say. And so I began, "It's me."

———

It was my third day in jail. Damp air hung in the cramped cell. The ground was hot, and the heat coming in through the small opening made it even worse. Exhausted and dehydrated, I languished in the corner. I heard footsteps approaching but thought nothing of them. I stayed in my place, brought my knees up to my chest, and curled up. The footsteps stopped in front of my cell.

I looked up. What I saw was a man tightly held by two other authoritative men, dressed formally. Even though nothing fazed me much in this place anymore, as I had already given in to my fate, I was shocked this time. The man, under the tenacious hold of the two officials, stared into space. It seemed as if he could see a ghost in my cell, so I looked back at him twice to see what he could see.

Taking in the situation, I tried to analyze how I might benefit from the men in front of me. I pondered the ways I could convince them to help me escape. There was nothing of the sort to be done though. All that was new was the cellmate I had acquired. I felt a glimmer of hope when the two men began talking. Their thick accents and voices uttered words in a far-off language. I shifted my eyes across the room. How could I use this to my advantage? I was fluent in the language they were speaking from the strenuous months of traveling.

Ever since I was a child, I didn't like meeting strangers. But war shakes you by the shoulders and disrupts the life you know and changes the person you were. I had talked to so many men of different faiths, witnessed innocent lives being lost, and had changed identities as well. I had literally transformed. It was ironic how I noticed this only when I was locked up and had the time to contemplate such matters. But now I knew that throughout these adventures, I had learned this one lesson: take whatever you can from your circumstances. If you can use your circumstances to your advantage, things can turn out to be in your favor.

As the two men continued talking to each other while glancing at me every now and then, I listened to them intently. The prisoner stood like a zombie waiting to receive orders. And I noticed a sharp difference. The two men treated the prisoner much more harshly than others. The dour man had marks and bruises on his face, as if they had beaten him up.

Did these two do it? I wondered. *But why would they do that? Did he commit a first-degree crime?* If so, then I didn't want him to share an already unlivable room with me.

My questions were answered when I heard one of the two officials snarl, "These fools from the Issa tribe always become discomfort for us. Can't they do something right for once?"

From all my years of studying Ethiopia's history and meeting a wide range of people, I understood the hidden meaning behind their claims. I got the hint—the opportunity that I could use as an escape. I found the rhythm.

Basically, the Issa and Afar tribes despise each other. They have remained longtime rivals and would use any available opportunity to degrade each other. I could guess from the eyes of the Afar men that they were passionate about their blood and tribe. They had an individual from the Issa tribe wrapped under their custody, and that was the reason behind the smug *satisfaction* on their faces.

As one of them asked, "Who's this?"

I steadied myself. Despite feeling worn out and broken, I answered in the Afar language, "It's me." These two words started it all.

I spoke confidently. There wasn't a hint of a foreign accent or mispronunciation that could cast doubt on my identity. I spoke like a true Afar man. Hearing me speak, the two men perked up like a wild animal noticing its first winter prey. Their eyes widened, and their heads tilted toward me. They whispered among themselves for a minute. Then, without any hesitation, they threw the other prisoner in the cell. His broad figure hit the dirty ground, and the thud echoed in the small confines of the cell.

I took a quick look at my cellmate. He was in the same position since they had pushed him inside. He appeared to limp. Curious, I reached out my hand to put on his back to check if he was even breathing. But I wasn't able to do so, as the two men dragged me outside the cell. One man grabbed me by the arm. He looked intently at me as if he were going to tell me his darkest secrets.

For a second, I wasn't able to grasp the situation. My body was very weak, so I couldn't even stand straight, and the man had to support me. His rough hands gripped my weak body. The other Afar officer next to him had been continuously addressing him as Captain, so I believed he must've been a high-ranking officer. And he truly proved that with his steady and solid grip holding me straight. My legs felt wobbly as my head spun. But I wasn't concerned about standing upright. I was finally outside the cell! I wasn't in jail anymore.

I saw the metal bars and could imagine what I looked like to an outsider staring out from behind them. Those bars didn't confine me in that instant, however. My vision was no longer constricted by the walls of the cell. I had wanted to feel free, even if for a second. And now, as I felt free, shivers ran up and down my spine.

Of course, I was still cautious about whether these men would figure out my actual identity and that I didn't really belong to the Afar tribe. So, I tried to avoid letting the situation overwhelm me. I had to take every step with careful thought.

"Come on now," the man said in a noticeably more passionate tone than before. The immense change in his attitude was staggering for me. I gave him a laugh and lowered my head.

"When did you come here?" He threw the question at me this time.

I smiled to myself for grasping the opportunity. By portraying myself as an Afar man, I had both individuals' attention. Their love for their tribe blinded them, and I was more than ready to use it against them.

"I came here three days ago. They gave me no water or food, not even clean clothes," I replied in their language, ensuring that I remained careful with the way my words came out.

The man sighed but nervously laughed. "I didn't know! Lord, three days in that place?" He pointed at my cell, where the other prisoner had replaced me. I could barely see the prisoner hunched in the corner.

At that moment, my stomach grumbled loudly. The sound was so loud that I put a trembling hand on my flattened belly. "Can I get something to eat?" I asked right away. Before I could start anything else, I needed to satisfy the hunger that had built up from three days of being deprived of food and water.

Hearing my request, one of the men left me and turned the corner. After fifteen minutes, he came back with a Coke bottle and a sandwich wrapped in cling film. I salivated as I looked at the meager fare before me, thinking it was heavenly.

I opened the drink. It was lukewarm, so I gulped it all down in one go. The bubbling sensation of the carbonated drink and the acidic feeling it left on my throat almost made me cry. I had never chugged carbonated drinks before. For some reason, it always burned my throat, but this time, I was desperate. I held onto the bottle as if for dear life. My grip was so firm that it appeared I was afraid someone would snatch it away from me.

After finishing my meal, I lifted my head only to see the concerned eyes of the two men standing before me. I thanked the man who had gotten me food. He put a reassuring hand on my head. All of this reminded me of how small I truly was. I was still a child, a boy in his late teens. I hadn't even hit my twenties, yet here I was, overwhelmed from just having a sandwich and a Coke. *What a life!* I thought. At this point, I was so skinny that my arms were like sticks and my waist seemed sunken in. It had taken just a week to break me completely. And who knew? It might take me years to piece myself back together.

"The name is Omar. Here," the man who got me lunch said.

Omar stretched out his hand for me to grab and lifted me up. I could feel a jolt of energy run through me from the food I had just consumed. My throat hurt, but I focused on Omar, who stared at me as if he had many questions to ask.

As I settled down and wiped my face, Omar began to ask me about how I had come to be in jail. I didn't have the right words to explain it all at first because I was scared of what I would end up saying. I couldn't arrange my thoughts correctly. What if they didn't believe me or just declared me a spy again? My heart clenched tightly. But I had to brush off the thoughts that circled my head and find my voice again. I needed to speak and inform them of all that had happened to me. My story needed to reach someone's ears. If they suspected me again, I'd just go back to jail, but if it worked out, I would begin my journey as a lonely yet determined refugee once more. I had to make a decision. I silently prayed to God to help me make the right one.

It was terrifying to think about the unknown possibilities and outcomes of my words because I had finally captured a ticket to freedom. I cleared my throat and began. "I want to leave this country, and because of that, I was imprisoned."

Hearing that, they looked a bit shocked, but as they considered me a comrade, they didn't ask more questions.

I went on. "I think you must be widely familiar with the bloodshed going on at the moment. I just want to ensure a safe and secure future for my family, so I planned my escape."

"So, you want to continue your refugee journey?" the other officer standing beside Omar inquired.

I nodded. "And for that, I would need to leave this place and reach the inner part of Djibouti."

After finishing my sentence, I immediately lowered my head, looking unconfident. "I don't think I'll be able to go there, perhaps," I said. To make my claim more convincing, I tried to cry. As they saw my slumped body and my tears, they turned sympathetic. I waited for one of them to lend a hand to help me get back up, and that is exactly what they did.

Omar pursed his lips as if he were in deep thought. Pacing to and from, he finally arrived at an answer. He said, "We can help you reach Djibouti safely."

I almost couldn't believe what I had just heard. I tilted my head so he would repeat his words. And as he did, I closed my eyes and immediately grabbed his hands. Thanking him with tearful eyes, I tried to express my gratitude.

"We'll go by boat tomorrow. It'll be a tough journey, so you'll first have to get ready. We'll give you a fresh pair of clothes," Omar said after detaching himself from my embrace.

All of it felt like déjà vu. The last time I had hope. I remembered how I had showered, gotten ready, and reached this place in clean clothes. Now, the same loop was repeating itself. I had a lot of expectations this time. I had been saved and given hope so many times. I felt grateful but still impatient. The thought of my journey failing again, leaving no chance for me to build a happy future for myself and my family, left me in shambles.

"We will reach it, right? There won't be any problem, right?" I tried to ask.

Omar quickly reassured me, "Everything will be settled. You'll see the light of Djibouti soon."

At that moment, I felt like a child who had finally gotten the chance to watch their favorite cartoons on a day off. I stood up, leaving the empty Coke bottle to the side, and followed the direction the two men took.

Before leaving, I threw a quick glance at the prisoner who was lying in the cell I was supposed to rot in. His chest was heaving, while unnatural voices escaped his lips. He turned left and right, remaining restless and unable to find comfort in the tiny cell. His gigantic body quivered. Looking at his miserable condition forced the food that I had just consumed to make its way up my throat. Almost gagging, I grabbed my throat.

I couldn't bear to think about the man's future. He would probably rot in that cell until his last breath. His family, friends, and people who were close to him would long for his presence, but he would not be able to free himself. I had manipulated my surroundings to my advantage, but tragically, many couldn't do the same.

Even though I did what was right for myself, guilt overtook me. The men in this place were criminals or thieves, but some had to be innocent. Just like me, they probably wanted to leave this country, which promised them zero growth, as well. It broke my heart. I was taking small steps toward a heavy fate. Even as I felt sorry for all the men in the jail, all I could do was move past them. It was the bitter truth that the only one I could save was myself—and that, too, only if I was lucky.

CHAPTER 10

The Journey to Djibouti

The morning wind swept past my face. The screeching cries of a faraway bird echoed insistently under the cloudy sky. The changing hues of the sky signalled that the muddy city would experience a slight rain shower. It began to drizzle, and the hidden sunrays eventually peeked out like children playing a game of hide-and-seek. Yet I didn't feel satisfied. I had always adored cloudy days during summers, but my bruised feet were in no mood for rain. Even though the heat had subsided and the dryness in my throat had lessened, I remained glum.

I could barely sleep during the night. My anticipation for the upcoming journey kept me awake, and I spent many restless hours staring at the ceiling. I counted sheep and even the number of cracks in the walls surrounding me but to no avail. The buzzing noise in my ears irritated me. There was an unreal number of flies and mosquitoes that tested my patience throughout the night. I fiddled with my blanket and tossed and turned, but sleep relentlessly eluded me.

As the night grew darker, I lay on the cold floor and stared straight ahead into the gloom. So many conflicting thoughts kicked up a storm inside my head, leaving me frustrated but hopeful for the day to come. I remained still and just thought about what would come next.

Somehow, I believed that taking small steps toward the boat would help me relax. But I was still so exhausted that whatever I looked at appeared blurred. Still, I took two deep breaths and tried to calm myself. It was important, and I reminded myself of how lucky I was to even get on this boat and journey toward a better life. Just spending three days in a rotten jail had left me worn out to my bones.

It was hard to even think of the possibility of spending more than two days in a prison cell that had removed me from the world and my identity. I looked here and there as my irregular heartbeat steadied and jumbled thoughts fell silent. I saw a bunch of men carrying wooden boxes. Their patient figures carried the boxes as if they weighed less than a feather. Their uniforms fluttered in the breeze, while their rough hands remained busy in the task assigned to them. None of them procrastinated or engaged in small talk. They meant business, as I could tell from their intense look.

Leaving the men to their work, I fixed my gaze on the giant boat that swayed restlessly on the water's surface. It was in perfect condition, with enough space to accommodate a dozen people. The exterior was white, and its sides were painted gray and yellow. The two men who would guide me toward the boat were conversing as they stood close to it.

Omar was neatly dressed in a clean brown shirt and glistening boots. The officer beside him had his hair slicked back; his hands were stuffed in the pockets of his well-ironed pants. I anxiously waited for them to call me so we could leave this place as quickly as possible. I didn't have a single good memory of this place. The most positive experience I'd had there was eating a French baguette.

Doubts began to creep their way into my head again. The urge to leave everything behind and go back also passed through me. For a second, I once again felt hopeless. I was thinking like a young man who craved peace but had been born in a country where human life was worth less than peanuts.

The image of my family and Martha drifted back into my head. I could still feel Martha's longing gaze and her beautiful lips shifting into a smile. Her slightly cold hands and the hazel in her eyes—I remembered everything as clear as day. I needed her by my side just so I could touch her rosy cheeks and feel her petite figure against my body. But the only thing wrapped around me right now was the dread of the unknown. The giant boat that would dictate my fate loomed before me ominously. As I lowered my head, I heard Omar's voice.

He was calling me. I puffed out air and walked toward him. I could not meet Martha this instant, but I decided the most I could do was move her to a safe place soon. A place where she wouldn't be fearful of running into the meadows, a place where love would outweigh trauma and sadness.

Boarding the boat, I looked one last time at the city behind me. I had no desire to ever come back. After a couple more men dressed in uniforms got into the boat, it began to move. Finally, I was on my way. It was yet another journey. I was fearful again; who knew what lay before me? All this time, I could have just been lucky. Maybe jail was a lucky conclusion. What if I got killed at the next stop? Nothing was certain. It was all in God's hands.

Despite the dark thoughts, I had no tears in my eyes. Was I numb? I wondered. There was the possibility that I had become indifferent to my surroundings because I had seen much more than I could withstand. But nobody could blame me for that. This time, I wasn't forcing myself to be optimistic. I had gone through the worst and luckily got out of the quicksand, but it was OK if I couldn't move past those experiences mentally. It was too soon, and I knew I had to give myself time.

It felt refreshing to remind myself that I, too, was a human who could break. Whenever I forced positivity onto myself, I raised my expectations. All this time of dressing up as a nomad and merchant and disguising myself and hoping I wouldn't suffer through the wrath of prison for the second time—I clung tenaciously to that hope. And if I didn't, I believed that it was genuinely a normal thing to do.

Nobody spoke throughout the entire boat ride. Everyone had solemn expressions on their faces. I wasn't in the mood to mingle either, so I just looked at the view, though it wasn't much. It was just dark blue water and tall trees everywhere. Somehow trying to motivate myself again, I thought about what the trees would look like in America. I thought of the parks there and of the wondrous flowers blooming everywhere. I had seen some of it on TV and felt jealous, as I had not experienced anything like it in real life.

Before the turmoil that my country went through, I was quite a patriot. Even if the streets weren't lit by luminescent streetlights or the roads were in bad condition, I considered it to be my home. And I still wanted it to be my home, but it would be ignorant of me to think I could make it there. It was no longer a safe place to live. America promised me a good life, and I wanted that. It would be much bigger and greater than anything I had ever experienced, and I tried to hold on to that thought to give me hope again.

Two hours passed, and the boat still chugged along. I began to feel tired. My legs felt crushed and lifeless from sitting in the same position since I had boarded. I fidgeted, and the Afar guard next to me took a hint. He collected his legs and slid a bit to the left. Thankful for the space, I adjusted and changed the position of my legs again.

Some people started to murmur among themselves, but it only lasted for ten or fifteen minutes. Another hour passed, and I lay my head back from the exhaustion. I was sleepy. I forcefully held up my heavy head and tried to make sense of my surroundings. The men had grown fidgety too and were staring at the infrastructure in the back. Upon asking, I figured out that we had finally arrived at our destination.

My heart started to beat fast, and the sleepiness evaporated. The guards got off the boat as it moored, and they helped me get down. As we reached the platform and steadied ourselves, the police were waiting for me. It all made sense because I was still a prisoner. Omar had probably informed them about my situation, so all I had to do was tell them I had relatives there who could prove my identity. The policeman looked at me with his dark, intense eyes. Scanning me from head to toe, he asked, "So you know you had been unrightfully imprisoned?"

Knowing the answer, I replied, "Yes, sir. They suspected me of being a spy and that I was faking my identity." I didn't want to get into the refugee bit yet, and I was hoping they already knew.

"I believe you're one of those who are leaving this country as a refugee?" the policeman asked, getting the gist of it from my situation.

Noticing his neutral tone, I made a quick decision to admit it.

He then hit me with another question: "I have heard you have relatives here."

I was glad there wasn't much explanation required on my part. Basically, my half brother's relatives had been living in Djibouti for a long time. "Yes! My half brother's family is here. I know where they live, and I can help guide you all," I said.

Convinced by my words, he dispatched a few people with me, and we started our journey in a jeep. We arrived at the place in half an hour.

The police officers asked me to get out; they encircled me and ushered me forward.

The house before me was huge. It had tinted windows and brick walls that gave it an overall grim aura. The police knocked on the door. After a minute, a woman, well in her late thirties and dressed in an off-white gown, opened the door. Upon hearing the information from the police, she decided to guide us in.

Making my way inside and passing by family pictures, I searched for someone—a face that I could recognize.

Finally, my gaze rested on a man sitting in the corner, busily chewing his food. His facial expression suggested he was worn out and tired. I could identify him straightaway, as we had crossed ways before. I knew him well. So, as I saw him, I pointed the finger at myself and said, "Hey! It's me. You know me, right? I'm Hanfere's brother!"

My voice came out a bit too desperate for its own good. It made me nervous, as it could make the policemen suspect me. The mysterious man lifted his face to look at me. He squinted his eyes and tilted his head. "I don't know you," he finally said.

I was speechless. This man completely forgot who I was and thought I came to Djibouti to spy on him. I had met him multiple times in my homeland. We had spent plenty of time hanging out as family members, and I even considered myself to be a close relative. "Why are you saying that?" I pleaded. The small hope I held onto was slipping away again, and I felt afraid. "You know me! It's Fikru!" I called out, emphasizing my name. He didn't look convinced, and it filled me with dread.

He said, "I have never in my life seen you." And then, as if he had regained his senses, he shot up and asked, "Are you a spy?"

I couldn't find any words. Again, my worth was reduced to this suspicion of being a spy. I didn't wish to go through that ordeal again, so I said, "How could I possibly be a spy, Hanfere?"

As he heard me say his name, he shivered and moved back. His eyes accused me as much as his words. "You even know my name, yet you're a stranger to me. You're a spy. I can't believe you won't leave me alone even when I'm in exile," Hanfere said. His eyes were bloodshot.

It confused me. I was more confused than terrified. There was no reason for this man to declare me as a dangerous stranger. My family knew him, and I still remembered him as clear as day. It disappointed me how he was now turning his back on me at the very moment that I needed his help the most. While writing this book, I learned that he died about two years ago. At the time, he feared the Ethiopian government was spying on him, but the allegations remain ridiculous. For what reasons, he threw me under the bus. I don't know even now, after all these years.

Still, I tried to reason. "Can you please just hear me out for once? I'm—"

But the policemen who were taking in the chaos took hold of me. It was the same sensation as before; I could not remove myself from their tough hold. Helplessness engulfed me as my hands were bound by men of authority. The cherry on top was when Hanfere concluded, "Oh, so you're the police? See, I told you this guy isn't right. Take him with you."

I shouted, "This is a misunderstanding, sir. He's lying! I know him."

I just wanted to convince them. Everything from the way they dragged me outside to the way they roughly handled me told me what was in store for me. I knew the same stinging atmosphere of jail awaited me. The police grabbed both my arms as viciously as they could and led me away. I stumbled, but instead of helping me get back on my feet, they pulled me up harshly. I was visibly shaking.

Once again, I had to pass the dark alleyways filled with desperate prisoners clawing at the bars. The guard fumbled with the keys to open the heavy metal door and throw me inside.

This cell was even worse than before. There was a rotten smell lingering in the corners. It felt as if someone had succumbed to their death there. The scorching rays of the sun exacerbated the restlessness and rising sense of dread that enveloped me. Sweat stained my clothes. I had barely consumed a piece of bread the entire day but still felt like vomiting my guts out.

This time, I had no one I could turn to for support. Even though I'd had little or no support in my previous experiences, things still felt different this time. They felt much worse. I believe it was because everyone was a stranger. I couldn't speak the language, so I was truly an outsider.

I was convinced that the chance to find the opportunity to defend myself like before was slim. The weather was so hideous that I closed my eyes and lay down in the middle of the cell, removing every layer of clothing that confined me. My surroundings were silent, and no one passed by; even the guard was busy elsewhere. There was no noise at all.

As time gradually passed, I could feel my body losing its strength. I couldn't lift my arms or move to another place. I remained stuck in a single position with just pain overwhelming me. Once again, it was like déjà vu. The last two times that I had been imprisoned, I was starved and warm. It was all coming back to me, and I resisted the urge to cry. With nothing but agony engulfing me, I tried to fall asleep.

The second day began. I had lost hope for receiving food or water because no one came near me. It was dead silent, like the last day. I didn't see the guard place trays of food for other prisoners either, so I gradually realized they wouldn't do so for me. There could have been many reasons why the prisoners were deprived of food. I could connect it to a shortage of food or the simple desire to starve the prisoners to death.

Whatever it was, I was slowly losing my sanity. I began to get sick from the lack of nutrients in my body. As the sky turned dark, I figured that I was ready to die because I did not feel even a glimmer of hope.

When the third day started, I was stiff on the floor. I could not move at all. As I took in the foul smells of the surroundings, I suddenly heard someone inserting keys in the cell door. I had no energy to even lift my face, but I glanced to see who was attempting to open the door.

An Afar policeman stuck his head in and motioned for me to get out. I shifted my weight to my right hand and tried to get up with what little energy I had. After I got outside, and the man locked the door, I collapsed on the ground, heaving loudly. Knowing I had barely eaten anything, the man brought me a cold bottle of Coke and a packet of biscuits. I quickly grabbed the Coke bottle and drank the bubbly goodness, coughing and choking in the process. Then I hastily tore open the packet and gobbled up the biscuits.

After I had eaten and recollected myself, the policeman asked me to stand up. I dusted off my clothes and followed the man with no questions. What else might happen? Even if he intended to murder me, it would be better than rotting in a prison cell.

A vehicle stood outside. The engine was running, and the man asked me to get in. I climbed into the back seat. Finally coming to my senses, I asked the man, "Where are you taking me?"

Without looking back but with conviction in his voice, he replied, "The concentration camp."

CHAPTER 11

Dikhil, the Beginning of Hope

The car drove down the bumpy mud road. The windows were rolled down a little, bringing comforting breezes that broke the tense aura. The man at the steering wheel looked straight ahead, his dark eyes hidden by his cap. Restless, I sat in the middle of the back seat.

My mind was blank, but from time to time, it was flooded with questions. It was difficult for me to comprehend where to begin. I breathed out, trying to regain a sense of control over myself. Both the men sitting before me had informed me that I was being taken to the concentration camp.

This decision was somewhat acceptable to me, as well as understandable because the police knew the ins and outs of my situation. As they were informed that I was an outsider, they had decided to shift me to a suitable place so I could live like a refugee. Many people in similar circumstances were provided the chance to leave jail and live in concentration camps. In the end, they gave just one final warning so the refugees did not break the rules and run away.

I guessed it all, but I was still fidgety and dying for another response from the officers. I longed for someone to open their mouth, utter a word, and shatter the terrible tension. Stuck in this frustration, I looked down only to see my red, bruised hands. I had rashes and calluses on my hands. My fingers were bony, my knuckles sore. As I stared at my palms,

I almost felt sick. The skin was shredded. The same palms that had held Martha with such gentleness and love, spun her in the air, and swayed her beautifully on a Monday morning appeared as lifeless as I felt.

The car ride wasn't doing me any good. The more I tried to ease my curiosity by shifting my attention elsewhere, the more negative thoughts attacked me. I needed to know the outcome of this particular journey. What was waiting for me at the concentration camp? This time, I closed my tired eyes and leaned my head back. I believed it was better to simply leave my concerns to God. He, with His utmost authority and power, would give me all the good things.

As I put my trust in Him, I slowly felt myself being soothed. The realization that I wasn't alone in my suffering and God would always be there for me brought me comfort and joy. I could breathe easily now; I could even smile. I laid my head back on the black leather seat and relaxed.

This calm spell did not last for long. After traveling 350 miles, we finally arrived at our destination: Dikhil. A giant white sign greeted us with the words "Dikhil Region De L'Unite." It had two designs painted in green and blue on the sides. There were carefully sketched images of palm trees on the lower corners of the sign.

Once we passed the massive pillar, it started dawning on me that I'd reached the place that would be yet another tiring journey for me. My heartbeat slowed as my chin quivered in fear. I was scared of the unknown again. I wasn't ready to withstand anything remotely scarring. However, that was inevitable. I was on my way to a place where beginnings were meant to be difficult and strenuous.

It was a path that gave no hope and only promised despair. There was never a positive beginning for an individual entering a concentration camp. Even if it was better than jail, I was still worried because I was simply tired of misery and hopelessness haunting me wherever I went.

During my journey from the start till now, I had made a small, unconscious promise to myself that no matter how tough things became, I would never stop searching for happiness. I didn't want to give up on my quest for a good life, so I still stretched my hand toward whatever joy I could find in dark places. I had to believe that those small moments of happiness would last through the harsh journey—at least till I reached the land of freedom.

With apprehension as well as hope, I looked around as the car kept moving. After a couple of minutes, the Afar officers began to talk to each other. Their bearded faces looked severe as they rambled on about the town we had just entered. One of the officers complimented the structures that stood along the road, while the other complained about the intense heat and fanned himself with a document.

I sat silent, of course. I couldn't figure out the right words to get them to respond to me. I knew they'd give me the same recycled answers. "Don't leave this town. Stay in the concentration camp, or you'll return to jail." Considering they had dragged me out of jail and were now putting me in such a camp, the one final warning had already started for me.

In a sense, I was bound like a bruised tiger in a filthy zoo. I bit my lip and stared out of the window again. After half an hour, the car came to a stop. The officers got out and instructed me to do the same. Limping slightly, I got out of the car and slammed the door behind me. I was in front of a police station. The grim aura of the building filled my flesh with goose bumps. I tried to think of a reason why we were standing before a police station, but no convincing answer came up. So, I asked, "Any particular reason we're here?"

One of the officers answered, "This is for your identification. We'll have you provide signatures and fingerprints."

I tilted my head as if I were still confused, so he added, "It is for registering you for the camp and gathering your data."

I nodded. They guided me inside the station. The smell of cleaning detergent filled the place. A couple of police officers roamed around. The officers told me to go inside a room located at the far right. They came with me. A man, well into his forties and with white hair, sat at the counter. He was intensely staring at a computer screen. Eventually, he greeted me. The officers explained my circumstances, and the verification process began.

The man placed a piece of yellow paper in front of me and handed me a pen. "Please sign here, flip it, and sign here as well," he instructed.

I rolled the pen onto the rough paper and signed it at the required places.

Like a programmed robot, the man then directed me to another spot. When I got there, I saw a machine before me. It had red and green spots where I had to put my fingers so that my prints would be recorded in the system. I felt irritated by the entire process. But then again, I had no choice.

After my prints were noted, the officers took hold of me and ordered me to return to the car. As I took in a whiff of outside air, I felt slightly better. So, I tried to start a conversation with the men. I asked, "Where will we be going next?" My voice was more upbeat than before.

Noticing the change in my tone, the officer at the steering wheel stared at me from the front mirror. His dull eyes stabbed me continuously. "Don't you know?" he scoffed.

I was taken aback by the annoyance in his voice. I gulped and lowered my head, shutting my mouth, but he began, "We're going to the United Nations. You can't just live like a homeless person in the camp, right?"

With wide eyes, I hesitantly nodded.

"So, what do we need to survive?" he asked.

He was puzzling me and having a great time doing so. Anger took hold of me, but I shrugged it away. "Shelter, food, water, clean clothes, sir," I said.

He said nothing, and his eyes remained expressionless. I sat there, confused as I tried to figure out his reaction. He just reverted his attention to the steering wheel. "You're going to get rations and a tent, but remember, if you ever try to escape this town, you will be thrown into jail again and much worse, even deported," he told me.

I sighed and leaned back. The torturous ride began again.

We arrived at the United Nations office in about forty minutes. I was provided with everyday items for my survival in the camp. It was all stuffed into a huge cardboard box, which was taped from all sides. It was unreasonably heavy, so I knew it contained heaps of food items ranging from rice sacks to oil cartons. At that moment, I felt grateful. My craving for small moments of joy was satisfied, and it was truly a refreshing feeling.

I was content to hold a giant box stuffed with edibles. For sure, my happiness was justified. I grabbed the box; it reminded me of how I had come a long way. I was overwhelmed by my new surroundings and the expectations I had. I also understood for a fact that my life in the tent would be hard, so I felt like I should prepare myself to face whatever may confront me. In my other hand, I held the white rolled-up tent. It kept slipping from my grasp, so I had to take care of it every minute.

After an hour of traveling, we reached the campsite. As I stood and looked at the sight before me, I only saw tents. White tents stretched as far as I could see. They swayed in the wind. I also saw people leaving the tents or snoring peacefully inside. I had never witnessed such a scenario before. It was both intriguing and daunting. I took a deep breath.

The officer noticed me squirm, so he said, "This is your new home now. Take a good look."

I wanted to scream in his face and ask him what else I was supposed to take in. I was about to lead a life of poverty and distress. I felt frustrated and angry, but the feeling was not intense; it was certainly not as bad as what I had felt in jail. I was a walking dead body in jail. The hurdles this place would pose couldn't top the depression I had felt inside the corroding walls of a musty cell.

"Thank you, sir. I will try to adjust well," I reassured the officer. I also threw a small smile his way so he could see that my intentions were pure and positive, even if they were the opposite of what he expected of me. When I look back now, I realize how naïve I was to want to fool a trained officer. He probably knew the secret I hid under that smile—the secret hope of leaving that place and settling in a far-off land.

Leaving the officers behind, I moved toward the camp. I carried the heavy box with the tent above it. I was also given a surprisingly warm blanket. It dangled over my right shoulder. Slowly, I took in my surroundings and peeked around. I saw women kneeling before a pot. Children buzzed to the sides. They were burning sticks to create fire to prepare lunch. The ingredients rested on a gray paper.

The innocent and giddy voices of the children as they jumped around spread across the field full of tents. Men appeared to be busy with their daily chatter or unloading their rations. I stood still for a second, not knowing where to begin. But after a while, I figured nobody was paying me any attention. I saw that I could easily move around without piercing eyes clawing at me and felt reassured. The grass crunched under my feet, and I heard the birds twittering.

The ration was heavy, so I put it in a corner so people couldn't look at it. Then I strolled around the camp to find a place for my tent. After five minutes of searching, I stopped. I had found a great spot for setting up my tent and organizing my rations. I chose a corner away from others because I preferred to stay alone. I opened the tent and began to put it up. Soon, I realized the process was difficult. Confused and slightly scared, I looked here and there for help.

Suddenly, a young man approached me. He had a slender build and wore a brown shirt. "First time here?" he asked.

"Yes, I just arrived. It is way too warm, and I cannot figure out how to open this," I told him.

He chuckled and grabbed the front end of the tent. In a minute, he'd prepared the basic structure of the tent and dug the nails on the corners. I was surprised at his speed and efficiency. It appeared that he had been living there for a long time. So, I decided to ask him about his story.

"Why are you here?" I asked.

He laughed. "The same reason as you. No?"

Then he threw a question my way. "What was your journey like till here?"

I fell silent. Tears were taking hold of me as I went back in time and was reminded of the hideous trauma I had withstood. I tried to shrug the emotions off. I realized I didn't want to explain my dreadful days in prison that had put my survival in danger. I also didn't wish to tell him how some of my own relatives had provided falsified information about my identity and contributed to my misery. I was horribly tired of it all, but something within me begged to release the frustration and just to let it out.

So, I didn't hold back and told the man the events that had led me to this place.

He listened intently and expressed shock at what I had endured. I wasn't surprised because my story was full of tragedy and misery. After that interaction, I decided to meet more people. Gradually, I met other Ethiopian refugees as well.

I narrated the same tragic story to them. They appeared surprised and shook their heads in disbelief. I had to enforce that it was the truth a couple of times. The other refugees also described their own turmoil and a fair share of hardships. They told me about their families and interactions with the officers, but nothing matched the crisis that I had suffered.

Those incidents were embedded inside my mind as a silk thread weaves carefully through a piece of clothing. The tents covering every corner and the helpless people lying on the dirty ground told me that this was my new life. So, moving on was the only correct option for me right then.

I took out a bottle of oil, burned some sticks, and then began to roast sardines. When the fish turned nice and crispy, I hungrily bit the top of a roasted sardine. The savory and salty flavor of the meat burst in my mouth, leaving hints of spiciness from the red pepper I had sprinkled over it. I gobbled everything in less than five minutes and washed it all down with a lukewarm cup of water. The food was enough to last me for the evening.

When the sky turned dark and the nocturnal animals came out howling, everyone remained busy preparing dinner. People roasted a range of food items on pans and pots. I fumbled in the ration box, finding the suitable ingredients for a healthy and tasty dinner. Fortunately, I had the recipe planned in my mind; I was going to cook a rice dish. I borrowed a pot from a neighboring refugee and began to fill it up with vegetables, oil, and rice. Mixing it up for half an hour, I carefully shifted it onto a paper plate and gobbled it all up. After eating, I made my way toward the refugees who lay awake and listened to their heartfelt stories while also sharing my tale with them.

This continued for a few days, but then I started to become nervous. I began to think about how I could leave this town and resume my original journey. I wasn't in an insufferable state but would be if I kept living there. I knew I needed to run away from this place as soon as I could. However, I couldn't do so because I was bound to this town by the law. And if they deported me or threw me in jail again, it would be game over for me.

Undeniably, both of these were terrible outcomes. However, at that point, I was only certain of the fact that I could not remain stuck there for long. The worst part of it was that I didn't have a clear plan in mind. I hadn't yet figured out how I could run away without being caught. I had to be careful. While I lay awake inside my tent, I obsessed over the ways I could remove the shackles and escape this place that now confined me.

CHAPTER 12

Refugee

A gentle wind blew inside my tent. The rays of sunlight touched my face, reminding me it was time to wake up. Rubbing my eyes, I swallowed and realized how dry my throat was. My left arm hurt; it seemed I had slept on it through the night. Before getting up and starting my life at the refugee camp, I just lay in bed.

Nursing my arm with my right hand, I reflected on how, even though the tent was uncomfortable, I had slept well. I had dreamt of nothing. None of the good memories of fun times involving my loved ones came to ease me. But I also didn't have nightmares of my days in prison. I tried not to think too much about the days I had spent locked up in different detention centers. The distraught faces of the prisoners and the brutal treatment from the guards still lingered in my mind.

It was a terrible memory, and I was scared it would haunt me in the form of nightmares. But it didn't, and I slept like a baby. It had been years since I'd collapsed on a bed—or a pile of sheets in my case—and just snored away.

I felt refreshed, so I left the tent with a beaming smile on my face. There were white tents stretched all over the field. The people who roamed around me had spoons and bowls in their hands. Their clothes were stained and torn in places. I was relatively new, so my garments weren't worn out yet. Seeing these people reminded me I would meet the same fate if I stayed here.

Even if this place was better than jail, it didn't promise me a fulfilling future. I would have died in prison if I hadn't got out, but I realized I could also rot to my death in this small tent with a false sense of security. There wasn't much of a difference if one thought about it.

I looked at the rations that lay before me and realized there was at least one difference now: I had food.

I fumbled through the giant box to find the ingredients for breakfast. As I examined each item, I realized that the rations would not last for long. I didn't let it bother me for the moment. I took out rice, oil, and an egg and began cooking. I lit the fire by borrowing some sticks from a neighboring refugee. The smell of rice and egg made my mouth water. I sprinkled a dash of salt and pepper and sniffed the masterpiece I had prepared.

As I was busy cooking, I looked out to see what others were doing. Some refugees were still lying in their tents, unbothered enough to not even shut the front flap of their living quarters. Kids played tag and ran around the tents. Their childish laughter filled up the otherwise quiet area.

Men sat in groups and chatted away. I wanted to do the same. I had talked with two people on the first day, but I wanted to hear more stories. Maybe some of us had shared the same fate: rotting in jail and then thrown in a camp. I barely had anything to do in the camp. My entire life now revolved around these tents, so I had to talk to these people.

I prepared my food and devoured it. Then I made my way to some refugees sitting in a circle. They were eating roasted sardines and chatting with one another. I sat down to the side and greeted them. They introduced themselves to me, and I did the same. Then we began to talk about our past and our reasons for ending up in the camp.

"Oh, so you've been to jail as well? That sounds rough!" one refugee, a tall but bony man, said. He looked shocked.

I just nodded and said, "Well, yes. It was tough, but at least it's all over. How long have you been here?"

They told me how long they'd been in there. Some had been there for quite a long while. They, by this point, had the town tattooed in their minds.

"You're new here, right? You'll adjust well," another refugee reassured me.

"Ha-ha! I guess. I finally reached Djibouti, but things went a bit downhill for me, as you can see," I said, pointing to my shabby tent.

"Wait, you've seen Djibouti throughout? We've been trying to leave Dikhil and reach the other towns in Djibouti, but that decision has been insanity." The tall refugee shuddered.

"Really?" I asked with genuine curiosity.

He sighed and stared at the ground in disappointment. "My comrades and I were on our way to Djibouti. It was such a difficult journey. I remember collapsing on the ground and my friend supporting me," the refugee explained. "We walked for fifteen days. Can you imagine? Going to Djibouti on foot? People died."

I gulped. I couldn't find the right words to say, so I only uttered a feeble "Sorry."

The man laughed and patted my shoulder. "There's nothing for you to be sorry over. This is just how it is. We risked our lives to reach Djibouti." He fiddled with the stick on the ground. He teased me by adding, "You're lucky you got to reach the country without sores on your feet!"

I just laughed along.

This initial interaction taught me a lot. If I needed to begin my journey toward America, I had to be stronger than I was. Everything was vague, especially my future. So, I needed to be resilient and levelheaded. Complaining about my time in the camp wouldn't do me good. I needed to adjust first, at least.

The next morning, I asked the refugees to guide me around the town. The entire day, we strolled around Dikhil, looking at the houses and shops. It wasn't exactly fun, but it wasn't terrible either. I liked how the morning wind caressed my face. There was a slight chill early in the morning.

The town was even smaller than I had imagined. It was so compact that we finished the tour in an hour. If you were familiar with the town, you could explore it all in half an hour. I didn't let that discourage me though. I enjoyed the scenery before me. There were small, uneven houses made of dirt and mud in specific locations. We also passed by a library and visited it. The other refugees were familiar with it, so they grabbed a book and took a seat.

I roamed around the bookshelves to see the various genres of the books that lay before me. While I wasn't an avid reader, I needed to find a way of easing my boredom. I touched the dusty books one by one. I grabbed two to three books, each of different genres, and sat down with the refugees. They were chatting and reading at the same time.

Sometimes they'd find a funny or interesting line or picture in a book that made them laugh their heads off. I took part in the conversations and tried to remain as lighthearted as possible. For a second, I believed that I forgot about the anxieties that were always tugging at me; I became one with the peace in my surroundings. I had fun, but I figured that this was my life at this point. There wasn't anything extravagant that I could look forward to. We could only go to small cafés if we had the money for it, and the library to pass the time.

Dikhil was an abandoned town where no one could even think of settling. It wouldn't be an exaggeration to say that it was placed in the middle of nowhere. In my childhood, when I heard stories of people stuck in a deserted place, it frightened me to no end. But now I was suffering through a similar fate. No monsters greeted me, and I encountered no demons—no, those were the fears of a naïve child—but the stillness and isolation of this place were nevertheless scary. And why would it not be? It felt like I was standing on the edge of a cliff, just a push away from plummeting to my death.

I knew the moment I tried to flee this town I would lose my life. I'd either rot away in prison or be shot dead on the spot. I had invisible chains wrapped around my body. The invisible noose around my neck tightened with each passing day. The more I thought about my situation, the more I realized I was living a real-life nightmare. I tried to make the most of each day, but the terrifying thought that I was bound to this town for life left me shaken. My life was going in never-ending, monotonous circles. It was always the same morning where I cooked myself breakfast and explored the same town over and over again with other refugees.

However, it wasn't always thorns and needles. I also made great friends along the way who lent me a shoulder, and I did the same for them. Despite our tight budget, we still tried to save up some money and spend time at the local cafés.

I clung to the small things around me to give me peace. The morning walks in the chilly weather and sunlight that suddenly shone through gave me hope. It helped me keep my conflicting thoughts in check. Every morning, I walked for a long time before starting my daily schedule of sitting at the library and chatting with the locals.

Aside from walking, when I didn't feel like sleeping, I slipped out of the suffocating tent to just sit and watch the sky turn. I felt consoled by the glint of the stars and the puffy clouds that passed by. But the moon moved me in ways I could not explain. I could stare at it till it was the only image engraved in my mind.

I had never been a lover of nature. Sure, I liked being in the outdoors, but I had never before found comfort in stars and sunlight and the moon. But now, everything was different. Nature had acquired a new meaning for me; it reminded me that my family and Martha were watching the same sky, stars, and sunlight. And through that, we were together. The realization that I was close to my loved ones through God's beauty helped me relax.

I still had doubts, and I still hoped to leave this dull, drab life behind. But I knew it would be hard to do so. I needed to stay patient and find coping mechanisms that would remind me I hadn't made the wrong choice. I never regretted the decisions I had made to reach this stage, but sometimes I looked back to see what I could have done differently. I easily got overtaken by regrets, so I had to opt for small ways of bringing back my original determination.

Then one day both my determination and hope came back when I ran into a relative on the muddy streets of Dikhil.

A month had passed since my arrival in the town and settlement in the camp. That day, I was out and about for my daily routine. On my way to the library, a man bumped into me. I looked back apologetically and asked if he was hurt. The man's face was turned to the other side, so I couldn't see his expressions. He had thick, short hair and a scarf loosely wrapped around his neck. As he lifted his head to apologize to me, he froze.

No words were exchanged. We just stood still and stared at each other like zombies. It was he who broke the tension. "Fikru, what are you doing here?" he said and extended his arms to welcome me.

I gasped in shock. The man before me was Pastor Alo Aydahis! He was a relative of mine, and it surprised me to see him here. He seemed to be even more surprised, as his mouth remained open in shock.

I eased his curiosity and said, "I can't even explain. It is a long story, but if I were to sum it all up … well, I'm here as a refugee."

Alo's eyes widened, and he took a few steps back. Without wasting a second, he asked me, "Why? What's the reason?"

I looked the other way so he wouldn't see me roll my eyes. I already felt tired when I thought of how I had to explain my awkward and painful journey.

I said, "Well, I'm trying to leave this country. I'm thinking of immigrating to America for my family and myself. I know you'd call it a stupid decision, but I really can't back off now, nor do I want to."

He nodded at my words. I was grateful that he could understand.

"I need to leave this place, but I just can't. If I try anything funny, well, I bet you know what happens to rebels."

"I can only imagine," Alo said, his voice gruffer than before.

I asked him to walk along with me. I was grateful for the cloudy weather, but after a minute, the unforgiving sun peeked out. Sweat beads formed on my forehead. I continued to walk with Alo. "How's your job going?" I asked him while I kicked a lonely pebble on the road.

He sighed and stretched. "It's stressful." He laughed. I chuckled along as well.

He shook his head and said, "Well, everything can be stressful. Being a pastor is a laborious job but very rewarding. It was something that I hoped to pursue for a long time too."

I listened but didn't respond.

"I think I've told you this before, no? When we met at your place? I don't know. I can't remember." He laughed once again. "My life is flowing as it is, and I'm not stuck in the middle." He stopped and added, "You are though."

I turned to look at him. His face was more serious than before. I didn't know what to say. He grabbed my hand and said, "Is there any way that I can help you? I think I can."

I felt a ray of hope force its way inside my despairing heart. I had another opportunity right in front of me, and I was more than ready to grasp it. "How will you help?" I asked.

He tilted his head as if he were in deep thought. Then he grabbed my shoulder and began, "You need to leave this place without getting recognized as a refugee, right? I can help with the identification process." He took out a pen from his pocket, clicked it, and smiled. "I can prepare a letter for you that might help you get back on track for your journey and leave this town behind."

I would get another fake identity. It made sense, but the thought of all the fraudulent identities I had taken made me laugh. Alo noticed and asked me why I was laughing. If only I could explain to him the absolute mess my life had been for the past months! If only I could find the words for it!

I thanked Alo for wanting to help.

"I can get it done in two days, and then we'll meet at the same location?" he asked.

I nodded. "I'd appreciate that."

Alo waved goodbye and left, leaving me rooted to the spot. I could've almost dropped to my knees from the relief of finding a possible way out. I was happy and hopeful after what felt like a long time. Even though things had not taken any shape, I thought I had a clear direction in front of me this time. The thought of the letter kept me going. The Lord was coming through for me yet again at a critical juncture in my life. Just when I felt as though I had hit a dead end, He opened up this new door for me.

Every day, my mind drifted away to a far-off place. I didn't talk as much as before and didn't read the books I had loved. I didn't go to the cafés, nor did I take my morning walks. I was wholly and utterly invested in the letter and the journey Alo had promised me.

In two days, I met Alo at the same place as before. He waved at me, and I waved back. As I went up to him, he showed me the letter.

"We'll be going tomorrow by bus. The paperwork is done. Just need to pass the checkpoint now," Alo reassured me. I sighed in relief, but there was still a lump in my throat.

Before even starting the journey, I was quite scared. If this went wrong, I couldn't come back to the camp again. There was no second chance. They would send me straight to jail. Yet I clutched the letter tightly in my hand and looked ahead.

The next day would decide whether I would stay behind metal bars or continue my adventure toward America.

CHAPTER 13

The Letter

Beads of sweat decorated my forehead. My head was spinning, and my heart rate seemed abnormal. I stared at the empty scene before me. The dark, lonely trees swayed in the wind, and the sun glared from behind thin clouds. Only a few people passed by us, all of them busy with their tiring routines.

Alo stood beside me, dressed neatly in dark pants and a caramel shirt. I turned my head to face him, hoping to start a conversation, but he was lost in his own little world. I was clutching the letter he had prepared for me. We were waiting for the bus so we could start our journey toward Djibouti.

Even though the rays of hope I had wanted were warming my heart, I was restless. At some point, I also thought of returning to the tent. I looked back a few times to consider my options. But I needed to take the chance. I needed to make the most out of this opportunity that had presented itself to me so unexpectedly. My gut kept saying that God was yet again opening another door for me. After a few more minutes passed, I could make out a huge vehicle heading in our direction. The bus was finally arriving. It was still far away, but Alo leaned in the big vehicle's direction as if he would jump and board it the minute it arrived.

The neutrality in his expressions subsided, and he glanced at me. "You seem a bit nervous," he said in his hoarse voice that I'd gotten used to.

Instead of shrugging and pretending to be stronger than I was, I sighed and smiled. "I am nervous, I must admit. I don't know what to expect, so I'm trying not to think much," I answered, the panic plain to hear in my voice as my voice cracked toward the end.

He clasped his hands together and said, "I understand, but you wanted to take the chance, right? The camp won't do you good. You need to get out of here." He looked at the ground, and a small smile spread across his face. "As a man of God, I took advantage of my situation to help a fellow brother out."

His words calmed me down way more than I cared to admit. Before I could say thank you or appreciate his help, the bus was right in front of us. We quickly boarded it, taking seats in the middle to the left side. The window was close by, and I was grateful for that. I could calm myself by looking outside as the bus moved—an old habit of mine.

The journey toward the checkpoint began. My do-or-die venture had commenced. Undeniably, I was content with sitting on the bus and traveling normally. I wasn't reduced to a label, nor was I considered a fraud. It felt great to travel as anything other than a refugee stuck in this town for life. In that instant, I felt like a common man who didn't have an invisible chain around his feet.

It was strange to dwell on such thoughts because I had decided to put myself at risk. I knew the consequences of my actions better than anyone else, but I couldn't help but think, *What if I didn't leave?*

This initiated a chain of questions in my mind. The first was: *If I went back, would I be happy?* If I was satisfied with not taking risks and living trapped in a small town, what about my family? How would they survive? What would be the point of risking my existence to escape from this war-torn country?

No, I couldn't go back anymore. I had absolutely no desire to go back and live a sheltered life where every day seemed to be a battle against the world. The Ethiopian blood coursing through my veins wouldn't stop me from pursuing something better, something less violent. I gulped and leaned back in my seat. Closing my eyes, I prayed for my family's health and safety, but before anything else, I prayed for myself.

I made sure my mind was clear of all my old expectations and hopes. I didn't want to feel disappointed again. I sat on that bus as a new person, someone who confronted his misfortune head-on. The bus ride continued while I tried to wipe my head clean of any possibilities, favorable outcomes, or hope.

As half an hour passed, I lifted my head to see what Alo was up to. His gaze was fixed on the road in front of us. Then I peeked at other passengers. Starting my life as a refugee truly taught me that every stranger is a walking story. There are unsaid words and tragic events hidden behind straight postures and constant smiles. They harbor brutal secrets. They try to suppress them in the deepest, darkest corners of their mind so they don't have to relive the painful memories over and over.

I am the same as these strangers; violent memories rage within me. I hope to get rid of them, but the reality isn't sweet and simple like that. It is terrifying and unpredictable. It laughs in your face, reminding you how silly it was of you to wish for peace.

Even Alo, who sat quietly beside me, must have experienced his share of traumas. He had always been upbeat about becoming a pastor. It was a dream he had been obsessed with since a young age. From the outside, one would think of how lucky he was to achieve his dreams. But people forget the hustle and hardships behind that success. I imagined a scenario where I finally reached America after months of suffering. I wondered, *Will people think the same of me?* That I was lucky to leave a war-torn country and make a safe home in a peaceful place?

I shuddered and looked the other way. I knew I didn't need to prove myself to any other stranger. If I overcame these painful experiences by myself and set foot in America, I'd appreciate myself. And nothing truly mattered other than that. I had started this journey for my loved ones and myself, and that's what I needed to focus on.

After a few more minutes of traveling, we finally arrived at the bus stop. I could see the checkpoint before me. Men in military uniforms proudly paraded in the small space. Their presence intimidated the passengers on the bus.

I was restless. I adjusted myself in my seat and met Alo's eyes. He nodded reassuringly, but I instinctively understood that he was nervous as well. He placed a hand over mine and murmured in an unconfident but soft voice, "It'll be OK."

Two government officers climbed inside the bus and investigated the identities of the passengers. I'd hoped for them to be a bit careless with the checking process, but to my dismay, they checked thoroughly. They even threw probing questions at individuals who could not prove their identity properly.

My legs began to shake. *What happened to your idea of facing the bad head-on?* I thought in frustration.

I oversaw the officers take in minute details, stare at the IDs for longer than necessary, and then move on to the next passenger. Throughout the entire checking process, I wanted to curl into a ball and wished I could just somehow disappear.

After moving through the people at the front, the officer reached me. His sharp gaze almost cut through me. He tilted his head in confusion. I was scared stiff, but I figured he somehow recognized me. Even after seeing the paperwork Alo had prepared, their suspicious glares didn't leave me.

The officer kept staring at me as if I had offended his great ancestors. I could feel the world stop right in that instant.

In a loud and angry voice, he called out, "Didn't we tell you not to leave? You're a refugee! You shouldn't be here!"

There was a lump in my throat. It wasn't surprising that he had figured it out. The town was smaller than ever. He must have seen me at the camp. It didn't matter how he knew me because he was ready to grab me and throw me off the bus. And I had no means of defending myself against two trained men.

I still answered, "What are you saying?" I tried to play it dumb at first.

His face remained stony. "Don't be a fool! You're hoping for a death wish by leaving the town," he said quite bluntly.

I felt embarrassed because the surrounding strangers were staring at me. Alo looked terrified as well but didn't intervene because the situation was out of our hands way sooner than we had anticipated. Whatever Alo or I said was not powerful enough to convince the men in army suits.

"Get up. You can't stay on this bus," the officer declared. He grabbed my arm with the utmost force and dragged me out to the road. I felt weightless in that instant. I was as light as a small rabbit, while the officer was a hungry lion, ready to devour me for lunch.

I was outside the bus before I even realized what had happened. The violet rays of the sun almost blinded me. I lifted my head to see my companion still inside the bus with a horrified expression on his face. Unfortunately, I was used to all of this.

The officers then began their interrogation. It didn't need to last for long because my identity was out in the open, and only misfortune awaited me at this point.

"We cannot send you back to the camp. It is unpredictable what you might end up doing," the officer claimed with his grip steady on my weak arm.

"What will happen to me?" I asked with barely any emotion in my voice.

"Well, you will go to jail again," the officer said, commanding me to follow him.

I passed through the dark corridors of a suspicious building. The officers accompanied me without uttering a single word. The silence was so grave that I believed it could choke me to death. The more I walked, the more I felt my legs wobble. We reached the cell I was supposed to be thrown in. Bad memories slithered inside my head like so many tiny snakes. The guard ordered me to enter, and once I did, he locked the gate behind me.

I just stood for a while, as if the events of the day had hypnotized me. The stained walls screamed at me, and the broken ceiling cast a dirty spell on my consciousness. I collapsed to the ground with a thud so loud the guard had to ask if I had hurt myself. The metal bars of the small window above screamed at me: *you are not free!* The toilet in the corner and the bed on my right left a disgusting taste in my mouth.

There were no bugs, but I still felt tiny insects crawling all over my body. I scratched and turned around in my filthy excuse of a bed. I remember crying so hard through the night. The next morning, I had swollen eyes to prove it.

A day passed. How much more time was I supposed to spend in this box? The awful stench of the cell tormented me to death. Someone had passed away in this filthy place. I could just imagine a man whimpering in the corner, his stomach empty, his senses diminishing one by one, and his cracked lips whispering to the wind. No one came to rescue him, and he died a sad death in the corner of a prison, alone in the last minutes of his life.

Shivers ran through me once I pictured myself in that position. The hope of settling my family in America and finally watching their beaming faces vanished into thin air. I felt empty. All I could do was stay in the corner, crying and breathing in the damp air.

I believed no one was as lonely as I was. Since childhood, I had loved solitude, but now I longed for my loved ones. I wanted to feel the warmth of their hands against mine. Hearing their laugh and looking at them smile— all of it seemed like an impossible dream. I spent another day tossing and turning and regretting every decision I had ever made to this point.

Throughout my time in jail, I also pondered the strangers and relatives I had met along the way. Their existence helped me move hills, if not mountains. They had good intentions in their minds, and if God had something different in store for me, it wasn't their fault. I appreciated the small, often courageous efforts they made to disguise me. Just remembering it all brought fresh tears to my eyes. I felt pathetic for not returning the favor and completing my journey safely.

I knew it wasn't my fault, but how could a man awaiting his death in prison not blame himself? It would be naïve of me to stay positive after having spent two days in jail without food. The guards were hardly ever on their seats, and the hallways were as quiet as a mouse. I spent another day alternating between crying and sleeping. Three or four days passed. And then I heard the gate open.

An officer stood in front of me. His face looked slightly worried, yet his posture demanded attention from me. I could not think at all. I just sat straight while he explained my situation to me. He began by asking about my condition. I just shook my head and pointed to my surroundings. The man understood even though I didn't say anything. He kneeled to meet my eye. He said with severity in his voice, "This is the final warning for you."

I looked up to face him. My eyes were crimson red, and snot dripped from my nose. The corner of my right lip was bleeding, and I could feel how foul my breath smelled.

"You understand what I'm trying to say, right? This really is the final warning," he repeated. "If you keep trying to run away, you'll become a danger and a nuisance to us. You're not keeping your word or ensuring us you're a safe man by continuously running away."

I listened to him silently because he was right.

He continued. "We don't give out chances so easily. You can consider yourself blessed because you're receiving permission to leave prison."

I sat upright. My frown was slowly disappearing.

"Don't get it twisted, however," he said and leaned in. He was almost whispering in my ear. "If you try to escape from this town, you won't only be deported; you can get shot and killed on the spot too."

Even in that numbed state, I noticed the change of tone in his voice. After telling me I might get brutally murdered if I dared to defy the system, he asked me to leave the cell. I got up with shaking legs.

"I can go back to the camp?" I asked.

The thickly bearded man nodded, dangling the long prison keys from his thick fingers. I wanted to ask him if he could provide me with at least a water bottle, but he walked away without a word.

I left prison again. My head was throbbing, and I could hear my stomach grumbling painfully. I took small and slow steps, hoping to reach the camp as soon as possible. Something broke inside me, but I was more than happy to leave the grim prison building behind.

As I walked, I felt tears running down my face. Conflicting feelings raged a storm inside of me. I was grateful to have left prison, but I was a prisoner to this town again. I was unsure about how I could ever reach America at this rate. But the only way to stay physically healthy and mentally at peace was to take things step by step.

Again, I had to search for an opportunity that could give me the wings to fly away from this town. I relied on that thought for comfort as I processed yet another disappointment of my life.

CHAPTER 14

Humanity Lives

It was painful to walk because of my torn shoes and sore feet. My throat was dry, and I felt like I would pass out any second. The air felt fresh; it was the only thing that pushed me to take one step forward at a time.

I felt hopeless even though I had been freed from jail an hour ago. Unsaid words were sitting heavy on my chest, and I just wanted to scream them into the wind. Leaving prison, though liberating, left me with many questions. I didn't want to feel ungrateful, but what exactly was left for me after I was thrown back into the real world again? Only the small town of Dikhil, which suffocated me to no end. I felt as if I were in sleep paralysis, and this city was the monster that loomed over me. I reached the camp and silently made my way toward my tent.

I tried to sleep the pain and hunger away. I was so numb that even crying felt like a waste of time. I wanted to sift through the contents of the ration box and prepare a meal for myself. I also wanted to greet my friends and just go to the cafés, enjoy a light lunch, and visit the library. But I had no energy left. I was so mentally and physically drained that I just lay in my tent lifelessly and closed my trembling eyelids against the terrible reality of my life.

The image of the officer squatting before me, ordering me to come out as if I were cattle and not a human being, haunted me. I also felt anxious as I recalled how my broken and hungry body had dragged itself to the camp

I despised so much. It crushed me, thinking of the different hardships I had gone through. I turned to my side, sighed, and forced myself to go to sleep.

When I woke up, my entire body was aching. I stretched out to the ration box with the little energy I had left. Finding some sardines, I fried and gobbled them down in a minute. Going outside, I looked around. It was the same scenery, the same people, and the same white tents. I figured this was going to be my life at this point. I saw my friends sitting in a circle, laughing with one another, and having a great time. I went over to them. What else could I do?

Just like that, my refugee life picked up after a brief but significant break. I began my regular walks around the town with my friends. I had the whole place etched in my mind. I was aware of every street, corner, and spot, no matter how small it was. I knew things more than I ever cared to know.

A month passed. I was still stuck in a suffocating, monotonous life. I just counted my days, as if I could die any day. It was during this hopeless and depressing point in my life that I stumbled upon two French female nurses who were new to the town.

They were talking in French and curiously looking around the town. I bumped into them during my daily walk. They got the idea that I knew this town inside out.

"Excuse me? Can you help us around here?" one of the nurses called out to me.

I froze in my spot and looked back. There was no harm in helping lost travelers, so I agreed to help.

"Oh, you want to go to a café? I know plenty around here. I'll guide you there if that's all right?" I said. I offered to assist them once they told me they were hungry and in need of rest. I conversed with them in English, as we shared the language. They spoke broken English, but we got our messages across. I guided them around the city and brought them to a local café.

"You can sit with us if you want," said the taller nurse once we went inside the café.

"Sure, if I'm not being a bother," I said, smiling as I politely accepted their offer.

"Not at all! We wanted some company anyway," she replied, settling in front of a table close to the entrance.

I drew out a chair for myself. I had been to this café a dozen times. The metal chairs, wobbly tables, the entire menu—I was familiar with it all. They weren't hungry, and neither was I, so we didn't order much. It wasn't even lunchtime, so we only got tea and some biscuits to enjoy the breezy weather.

As we munched on the biscuits and sipped our warm teas, a sudden thought emerged in my mind. I knew that these people were travelers from the way they were unfamiliar with Dikhil. They probably had other areas to tour as well. I needed to know whether these nurses would go to Djibouti.

Police had given me the final warning, and if they caught me again, I knew for sure they would put me in jail for life. But this opportunity tugged at me. I thought this time things might be different.

As the two women with me chatted happily with each other, I took a deep breath and asked, "So you're traveling to many more places, I suppose?" Sweat beaded my forehead. I had no reason to be nervous, yet I was sweating. Maybe it was because I was scared they'd say Djibouti wasn't on their travel list.

Before the nurses could reply to my initial question, I threw in another question, as politely as I could, "Will you be traveling to Djibouti as well?"

The women didn't throw awkward glances or question my curiosity. They just laughed and answered, "Yes, we are actually. We will go there next week hopefully."

In that instant, I could feel the knot in my stomach untie. Without giving it a thought, I blurted out, "Is it possible if I can go with you? I have to go to Djibouti."

After a while, I realized what I had asked. I shouldn't have asked them that because I knew I wasn't ready for their response. I started to become restless, but their reply was beyond my expectations.

"Sure, you can," one of them replied as they looked at each other and agreed to my offer.

I was dumbfounded. Before I could ask the obvious, one of them clarified, "We can tell you live as a refugee here. If you were to leave, we would have to hide or smuggle you through the checkpoints somehow. I believe you don't have a problem with that?"

I knew I would be fine even if they taped me to the top of their vehicle. We continued to chat for half an hour and got to know each other well. I figured I could trust them. They were humble and helpful people who understood that a young soul was trapped in this terrible nightmare and wanted nothing but to get out. As they got to know me better, they expressed their empathy and appeared even more committed to supporting me. They had the resources to lend me a helping hand, so they agreed to take a chance with me.

Again, the hope came surging back. I was frightened and content at the same time. There was this constant thought at the back of my brain telling me everything would fall apart, whereas my guardian angel kept telling me there was no harm in taking a chance. If I let my fear envelop me, I would become a prisoner to this place permanently. And I would leave my family disappointed and heartbroken. That was the last thing I could ever make myself go through. So, I was ready, determined, and prepared for the worst this time. There were no thoughts of *What if I get caught again?* I just needed to take this chance.

"We're leaving next week. So, it's better if you see our house and memorize its address. You must come to our place to leave with us," the nurse sitting beside me said, breaking my stream of thought. "It's not that far from here. Once you know the exact location of the house, you must get there at 5:00 a.m. next Wednesday by yourself. The earlier, the better."

I didn't have the energy to ask further questions. I just uttered, "Will we go now?"

She shrugged with a small "Why not!" and we were on our way to the location.

Throughout the walk, I noted down the lanes and streets so that I could reach the house on time the day of my escape. Their house was big with fancy windows on the front, while the main gate had designs carved all over it. After confirming the address a couple more times, I bade them farewell and returned to the camp.

I don't think I slept well the entire week. Every day, I counted down the days till the beginning of my risky journey. I never said a word about it to my friends, nor did I mention anything remotely close to escaping. I hadn't told them when I went with Alo either. Though I trusted them and considered them good companions, there nevertheless was a line that I wanted to draw out.

We were all refugees living in a camp where our tomorrows were blurry and unpredictable. I was unaware of what these people would do if they figured I had a chance of running away. I felt terrible for thinking such things, but I couldn't resist because it truly was every man for himself.

The week passed as quickly as I had hoped. I woke up on the day I had to leave for the nurses' house. I could hear the buzzing noises of some faraway insects and small sounds of people snoring. Some people slept outside their tents if the weather was warm, so that was why I could hear them. I carefully left my tent, making sure the silence remained intact.

I stumbled a bit and immediately cringed, afraid that I had woken someone up. I looked around, and the place was as still and silent as a graveyard. I let out a sigh of relief and left the refugee camp.

My surroundings were dark. The tall forest trees loomed over the streets while I ran to the house that could single-handedly decide my future. The roads felt abandoned—no one passed me. I felt so free in that moment. I was on my way to a place where I would rebel against the system—the system that had confined me to a single place because I wished for a life free of hardships. The feeling of resisting such a system made me feel whole.

I ran into the night with determination and commitment in my heart. This time, I was convinced I needed to get everything straight and just leave this town once and for all. I needed to defy the officers who wanted nothing better than to throw me in prison. I needed to free myself of the title of a Dikhil refugee.

So, I ran toward that house as if my legs had never run before. About half an hour later, I stood before the gate of the house. I knocked loudly on the door and just waited. I tried to catch my breath and looked ahead with eyes intense with the desire to escape.

One of the nurses opened the door for me and welcomed me inside. She stood beside me as if she were ready to explain the entire situation to me. She didn't leave any room for tea or greetings; she got straight to business. "This is the Land Cruiser you'll be traveling in, and this is the place where you'll be sitting," she explained, motioning to the back of the vehicle.

"I'll be hiding you with the help of these," she added, pointing toward the blankets and boxes lying at the corner. She gave me a smile to calm my nerves. "All you have to do is stay as quiet as possible. If this works out, you will finally see the light of Djibouti."

I smiled back at her. It wasn't the usual smile that I pass off to kind strangers. It was a smile that meant I had been hopeless after so many days of tossing and turning in a tent, and now I felt so happy that I couldn't breathe. I also felt the need to cry—but not yet. Not till I left this town.

After loading the vehicle with the luggage, they called me over to set up my hiding spot. They asked me to lie down while they placed boxes all around me and covered me with sheets and blankets. It almost appeared as if I were part of the luggage at the back of the Land Cruiser. This was great because the more ordinary everything looked, the better chance we had of fooling the officers.

The nurses got inside the Land Cruiser and double-checked their stuff and my hiding spot. Then we began our journey toward the checkpoint. I couldn't see much except for the morning sunlight filtering through the light blankets over me. I was stuck in an uncomfortable position, and it was hurting my back. But I tolerated the pain and discomfort and just closed my eyes, shutting down my racing thoughts as well. The ride was bumpy because of the poorly constructed roads. My head hit the box beside me many times. I heard slight murmurs from the front of the vehicle as the nurses talked, but I couldn't make out the words.

Finally, we arrived at the checkpoint. I heard sounds of officers conversing with the men in front, confirming their IDs and ensuring they weren't spies or refugees. Once we were cleared and ready to drive away, another officer came close to the side of the vehicle. He asked to lower the windows. When I felt the car come to an abrupt stop, anxiety flooded over me. Why were they stopping us suddenly? Had they figured out I was hiding in the back? I began to overthink it all as I remained cramped in that small space.

"How can I help you, sir?" the woman at the steering wheel asked, blinking her eyes unnaturally.

The officer looked her in the eye and replied nonchalantly, "Can you give me a ride? I have an urgent business close by. It's OK. I'll sit at the back."

The nurse was hesitant and visibly panicking. That fright could be felt in her words. "N-no, you cannot."

The officer, with his piercing gaze and intimidating outfit, stared at her in confusion.

"There's no space in the back because of the stuff we hoarded there. You can sit in the front with us," the other French nurse said, breaking the tension.

The officer shrugged and jumped inside the vehicle. All I could hear were muffled sounds. I couldn't make out the actual words exchanged between him and the women. But I felt the issue was settled, so my anxiety subsided. We continued our journey toward the next checkpoints. It had gotten reasonably bright outside, as I heard birds chirping and the noises of busy vehicles.

Despite how I enjoyed listening to the birds sing in the morning, I couldn't indulge myself in nature's beauty. I feared the officer sitting in front of me. I could feel his presence and sometimes even understand what he was saying to the two women.

It was scary thinking that if he checked the back of the Land Cruiser because of suspicious activity, we couldn't even stop him. He had all the authority to do so, and if we objected, he could use a weapon against us. We weren't heartless enough to kill him if he figured out our scheme, nor could we tackle him, as he would spread the word once we left. Declining when he'd asked for a ride in front of other officers would have been a death wish as well. So all we could do was pray he didn't suspect someone was hiding underneath the cartons and blankets in the back.

After ten miles, the officer asked the driver to stop the car. He had arrived at his destination. He thanked the two women and eventually went along his way. The car felt lighter, so I figured the officer had left. I sighed in relief, and so did the nurses, because they were just as stressed out.

We hit the road again. The ride was more relaxing this time. Five more minutes passed, and the driver pressed down on the brakes again. It confused me why they had stopped again, especially in the middle of the road. They got out, came up to me, lifted the blankets, and asked me to take a breath of fresh air.

It was silly of me to forget that I needed to eat, drink, and rest properly as well. I was so focused on leaving and so content with finally passing the initial checkpoint that I didn't even bother to consider my physical condition.

"You need to refresh yourself. We still have a long way to go." The nurses prayed and then handed me a chilled can of Coke and a pack of biscuits.

"Thank you for being so considerate," I said, feeling tears well up. "All of this help truly means a lot to me."

The women shot a friendly smile my way. While I ate, they silently stood at the corner and prayed for a safe journey. It is truly amazing what the prayers of faithful believers can accomplish. And there was absolutely no doubt in my mind that God had sent these two women into my path to achieve His purposes in my life.

The Land Cruiser was parked to the side. I munched on the biscuits, overlooking the wide landscape before me. I wondered if Martha was looking up at the same sky and thinking of me. Knowing that Martha was out there waiting for me was enough to energize me even more than the food in my hands. Once my belly was full, my eyelids felt heavy.

The engine started. I immediately covered myself in the blankets and continued to hide. In that uncomfortable position, I felt my eyelids droop. I fell into a deep slumber. The next checkpoint awaited me, and I was oblivious whether I would pass it or become a prisoner for life.

CHAPTER 15

Northside, in the Horn of Africa

I woke up from a deep sleep. I don't think I had slept that well in the past couple of months. I rubbed my eyes and wiped off the drool from the corner of my mouth. I had spent the entire time curled up in the same position, and my back and neck ached. I peeped through a small tear in the blanket to see the sky dripping in warm colors. I had gone to sleep in the morning, but it was afternoon now. I had been asleep for a long time.

Yawning and trying to stretch in the little space assigned to me, I tried to find a comfortable position. The journey ahead of me was long. We still had a checkpoint to cross, and for obvious reasons, I was trying to avoid thinking about it. I was sick and tired of panicking from the knowledge that if they caught me, I would land back in prison.

I closed my eyes tightly. This wasn't the time for getting discouraged. I still had a checkpoint to clear. I adjusted my back, hoping to camouflage myself in the surroundings. Luckily, the ride wasn't too bumpy.

After traveling for three hundred miles, we finally arrived at another checkpoint. Again, the nurses were subjected to a series of questions, while the officers stared at our car suspiciously. I could almost feel my heart escape my chest cavity. A few more minutes passed as the interrogation continued, and they asked us to move ahead. This was the last checkpoint, which meant that we could now officially enter Djibouti!

Tears streamed down my face as I wept silently. The car continued toward the city I had so badly hoped to reach for so long. I could only bury my face in my hands and cry for everything it took to get here. I had finally accomplished the one thing that I had wanted for months. I had no words to explain the joy I felt once I realized I wouldn't have to wake up hopeless in the middle of the concentration camp, roam around with my friends for hours and hours, and repeat the tiring cycle the next day.

Throughout my journey, when I was frustrated and dejected, only one thing kept me going: my family and the hope of providing them a secure future. I always thought of my loved ones. But this time, I cried for myself. I cried tears of joy for achieving what had appeared impossible for months, so grateful for how far the Lord had brought me. We drove for another half hour, and the car came to a stop. The nurses moved the boxes and blankets so I could catch a whiff of fresh air.

"It was a long journey, but I'm glad we could finish it with no hurdles," the woman said to me as she fiddled with the blanket in her hands.

I smiled and nodded.

She patted my back and said, "Don't worry too much. I hope you safely reach your destination." She looked around. "It will be difficult from here on, but I know you'll be able to make it through."

I sighed and replied, "I guess, but getting here was the first thing in my mind. At least I have left that concentration camp behind."

She chuckled. "That is true. We can't help you from now on. You are on your own."

There was a hint of despair in her voice. She must have felt sorry for me, as I was a starving youngster ready to begin yet another journey with no one to rely on but myself.

There was remorse written on both the nurses' faces, as if they wanted to help me further. Before I knew it, they handed me a note of 5,000 francs, Djibouti currency. I stared at it, not sure whether I should accept the money or not. One of them reached out for my hand and closed my fist around the currency note. "This is the most that we can do for you now. We wish you good luck for the future," she said.

The other nurse shot a tender smile my way, so I knew I had to accept the money. It was a kind gesture, and I thanked them. They gave me a pat, bade me farewell, and hopped inside the car to drive away.

As they left, my senses finally revived. I realized I was alone with no luggage and nothing at all to my name except for the money the nurses gave to me. I looked around to make sense of my surroundings and figure out my next step. I must have walked a good ten feet when I came face-to-face with a man whose face left me in utter shock. It was unbelievable that I met him again. I thought I would never see him, but fate truly works in mysterious ways. Or should I say, God does.

It was Alo. He appeared more surprised than I was. He blinked twice to bring himself back to reality. Then he grabbed me by the shoulders, almost screaming in my face, "How are you here? How did you make it here?" He kept repeating the same question again and again.

I laughed and said, "I know. It is strange seeing me here considering what happened, but some kind strangers helped me out."

"What? Really? And you passed all those checkpoints?" he exclaimed. He was full of questions.

I sighed and explained how I met the nurses and how they arranged the entire escape with me. I also told him that this was the smoothest escape plan, except for the one where I disguised myself as a nomad.

After hearing my story and connecting the dots, he took my hands in his. "So, you're alone in this city now?"

I gulped and nodded.

"I can't believe it! This isn't OK!" Alo said.

He stared at the ground to recollect his thoughts and then continued. "I have a place you can stay, but it's not my house."

Looking at my face, he told me, "It is a friend's house. You can stay there for a night. We'll arrange something else after that."

This offer was better than sleeping on the streets, so I complied. The day was ending, so he took me to his friend's house, where I would stay the night. The place was tidy and neat. It had the essence of family and comfort. I saw that in the portraits on the walls and flower vases on tables. It reminded me of my house and family. I longed to see my family again. I had gone through absolute misery, and I just wanted a loved one to hug me and say kind words to me.

Unfortunately, I was still in the middle of this risky journey, where I had to plan out all my steps. I no longer remembered what it was like waking up in the mornings without my heart beating like I had just run a mile. I felt anxiety every morning, and I daily prayed for the voices in my head to calm down. The voices kept whispering that this journey wouldn't end how I hoped it would.

Alo sat cross-legged on the sofa, talking to his friends. I roamed around the place to ease my boredom and anxious thoughts. I didn't want to join the conversation yet because I was tired from hiding in the back of the Land Cruiser for so long. I wanted to straighten my back and move around to subside the pain of staying in a single position for hours and hours.

As night fell, we went to our room and arranged the bed. I was sharing a room with Alo. He appeared tired and wanted to sleep as quickly as possible. I didn't want to lie down yet, so I just let Alo occupy the bed because he was dozing off already. I just sat there contemplating the adventures that had brought me to this point. All of it felt like a cruel prank. It felt as if someone had placed me in a nightmare and subjected me to torture just for the fun of it. I knew it was nothing like that; whatever had happened was a consequence of the conscious decision I had made to flee and find a safe place to live.

Despite everything I had suffered, I was satisfied with my actions. I had challenged myself and the system to strive for what was important to me. I needed to see everything in a positive light to not lose my sanity and myself. I tried to remember the days when I was given food after several days of starving or when I had dressed up as a stranger to leave one city and then the next. These felt like fond memories leading to something great and fulfilling. And I prayed that my hopes would at last come true.

The people I met, memories I made, and even hardships I faced made me resilient enough to beat all the odds and be in the city all those officials had kept me away from for so long. Finally, I wore a smile on my face.

The next morning, Alo told me he was taking me to a missionary library, where I could stay safe for a while. He explained that I would be staying in a roofless compound inside. Alo made his way toward the person in charge. He was sweeping in a corner, and Alo called out to him.

The man had broad shoulders and a wrinkled forehead. Though he appeared as if convincing him could be difficult, he listened and considered the request of me staying there. Alo informed me that I would help the man with the daily tasks of sweeping, doing the dishes, or watering the plants if he allowed me to stay in the compound. I had no problem with that because at least then I would have shelter and wouldn't have to sleep on the pavement.

"Make sure you take boxes and cartons with you so you can use them as a mattress. The ground here is hard, so it'll hurt your back if you lie on it," Alo told me. He showed me the area I would stay in. It was better than my previous shelters. There was enough space to stretch my legs and sleep comfortably if I put cut cardboard boxes on the ground.

Though flies and other insects were crawling around the place, I wasn't bothered by that. I had been in worse places. I just didn't want to sleep on the streets because I was worried about getting beaten up or robbed of the little that I had. The people out there didn't show mercy even to the poor and helpless. But I couldn't call such people atrocious because everyone suffered from the consequences of the war. It wasn't surprising that people resorted to harmful options. In the world we live in, it isn't strange to see people become selfish.

I bade Alo farewell. He said he would keep meeting me, and I was thankful for that. And just like that, my life at the library began. It wasn't exciting or impressive. It was just the usual fight for survival. Every day, I would wake up on top of cardboard and cartons. I didn't have any spare clothes or extra money except for the money the nurses gave me. I would walk around the city, looking at the houses and infrastructure to see what it offered. It was a splendid place, and the citizens were friendly.

I had to hide my identity. I didn't give in to the curious questions of others and just kept lying every time I had to answer them. I wasn't always skilled at pretending. This was why I felt I couldn't safely complete this journey. During the time I had spent in jail, I had blamed myself for not being competent enough to escape imprisonment. There was always this lingering thought in my head that I could have done better, and the looming word *why* kept terrifying me.

After spending a few days peacefully, I felt better. The intensity of the negative thoughts subsided because I knew I was out of the stage where everything was unknown. I was in this city preparing my next move. My life here wasn't as burdensome as my previous experiences. I knew I had set the foundation for everything and just had to apply for my refugee card and status, which could help me travel elsewhere.

Every day, I rolled around in the compact space provided to me and helped around the library. I barely used the money the nurses gave me; I kept it safely tucked in my front pocket. I didn't want to use it up unwisely, so I bought very little food every day. I ate once or twice throughout the day and always opted for simple dishes like plain rice or soup. I enjoyed such foods. The dark days of my past kept me humble. I knew how lucky I was to at least have food because I had firsthand experience of what it felt like to starve till my stomach hurt.

So, this was all my life. I cleaned up the library in the morning and had warm goat soup for dinner. As this routine continued, I knew I had other things to do as well. I wanted to apply for my refugee status, so I had to visit the United Nations office.

I decided on a day and visited the office. Alo accompanied me to show support. The place had long corridors. A strange smell of cleaning detergent hung in the air. Many people passed by me, their faces looking stern yet worried. I could tell they had come to apply for the refugee card too. After asking for directions, we arrived before a long line. Some had paperwork in their hand, and others impatiently awaited their turn. I quietly stood in the line, noticing a couple more people line up behind me. The line was so crammed that I could smell the person in front of me. I looked ahead to see how much more I had to wait.

People were chatting, laughing, and crouching down. The place was noisy. I disliked crowded spaces, but I had to bear with it for just another hour. Luckily, the processing finished quickly for the people in front of me, and I got the chance to move forward.

My turn came, and I was asked to fill out an extensive form. They threw two questions my way, and I answered them as truthfully as possible. After receiving my information, they said they would inform me about the status a month later. I hoped to be selected. I had no clue what their selection criteria were. I thought I was an open book before them and emphasized my family and Martha throughout the session. I assumed that if they knew I had a family to feed and a lover to go back to, they would consider me as a worthy candidate.

I was hopeful but slightly anxious at the same time because four hundred people had applied for the status. The odds of me getting selected were slim, but they were not impossible. So, I prayed for a better outcome every single day. I believe I grew closer to God through this journey. I picked up the habit of quietly praying in my head when things felt a little out of control.

Every time I faced a difficult situation in my life, knowingly or unknowingly, I prayed to God. Now, my journey had finally brought me to Djibouti's United Nations office to complete the procedure for refugee status.

I knew everything happened for a reason. Sometimes my hope would crumble, but I understood that God meant well for me. Proceeding with this mindset really helped me calm my nerves and take situations one step at a time. So, I figured that even if I wasn't selected, I would try again until I received the result I wanted. Even if I felt hopeless for a moment or two, I knew God would help me. I was not ready to give up.

A month passed, and my positivity and hope manifested into one of the greatest achievements of that time. My application for the refugee status was accepted! I went to the UNHCR office to check my name. I almost couldn't believe that I did indeed make it. I told Alo the great news, and, the enthusiastic and caring companion that he was, he replied with much delight. The insane part of it all was that I was one of the few sixty-one people whose applications were approved.

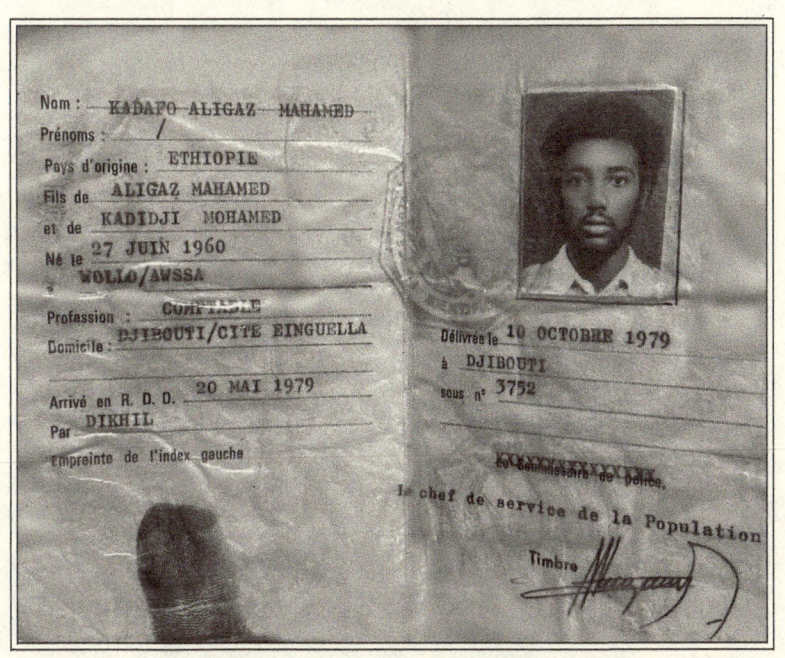

UNHCR refugee identification card

It would be a mistake to say that I was merely excited. I felt as if I had come full circle, and my hard work and commitment were finally rewarded. The fact that I would acquire a refugee card and become eligible for traveling to other countries if I received a scholarship or sponsorship made me feel light as air. Now, I wasn't just building the foundation of my journey; I had built it! It was time for me to color it, fill in the gaps in my journey, and finally call it an end.

After celebrating the news quietly in that small space in the library I had to myself, I looked at the scene before me. I had a bowl of piping hot soup in one hand. As I ate it, I looked at the golden sunset turning the sky into a masterpiece. At that moment, I knew that I wouldn't have to rely on a distant sky to feel Martha's presence. I was closer than ever to finally feeling the warmth of her hand and starting a new life with her in a new country.

CHAPTER 16

Hey There, Fikru!

The chirping of the birds forced me to open my eyes. I put a hand on the cardboard box below me and lifted myself. I was immediately greeted by the scorching sun. I placed my arm over my eyes to block the bright rays. I yawned and tidied up my little space. I straightened my shirt, ran my fingers through my tangled hair, and washed my face with the garden hose. I was accustomed to everything at this point. It felt strange thinking how I first believed I wouldn't be able to adjust to this place. Now I knew every spot of this library by heart. And why would I not? I had spent six months in Djibouti, after all.

After receiving my refugee card and officially being recognized as a refugee by the UNHCR, I decided to live there till I could find a better opportunity. I didn't consider my life there to be worse than what I experienced in the past, but considering I barely had any money, it wasn't exactly the most satisfying experience.

Every day was simply a fight for survival. I didn't dislike that because I knew how to survive by this point. Living in a roofless compound wasn't a big deal to me. I had my past to thank for remaining dauntless. It was horrendous, but it had made me humble, grateful, and resilient.

I always began my day by strolling the streets. I wouldn't greet strangers or window-shop often. Just walking around in peace was enough to help me collect my thoughts and pass the time. I walked by busy cafés, engaged strangers, and modest houses.

Once, I was so focused on my surroundings that I didn't notice someone call out to me. A woman was calling out my name repeatedly, almost as if she had known me for years. She kept saying, "Fikru! Fikru!" I was hesitant to turn around and greet her. The fact that she was familiar with my name meant I must've met her before I reached this place.

During the interview for the refugee status with the UN, I realized I had to change my name. I needed to show my credibility to connect the dots of my journey. Hence, I showed myself as someone of Afar descent and gave out the name Kadafo during the interview. My story would be flawed if I decided to blurt out the complete truth. Despite being as truthful and open as possible with the agency, I had to make sure that I wouldn't lose my one chance of receiving a refugee card.

I was befuddled about how this woman knew my real name. I turned around to greet her. I stared at her with uncertainty because I couldn't recognize her at all. The woman took big steps toward me and came near. As she drew closer, I finally identified her. It was Hasnaa. She used to work as a maid at our house in Ethiopia. I always remembered her as a kind and bighearted woman who tended to the children and respected the family. She was startled, bumping into me in an entirely different country.

"How did you get here, Fikru? Why are you suddenly in Djibouti?" she asked me with a voice full of concern.

Every time I met someone familiar in the middle of my refugee journey, they would ask me how I got there. I was unsure as to where to begin this time, but I found my voice and said, "I am here as a refugee. I'm on a quest to America."

She inclined her head and responded, "I see. I never imagined this to happen though. It's beyond me how you even reached this place. There's always tight security around these checkpoints."

I didn't go into the details of my adventure and instead asked her why she was here. I was just as shocked to see her in Djibouti.

"Oh, me? I came here legally for work. I came here a long, long time ago actually!" she answered with a welcoming laugh.

"Are you going somewhere?" she suddenly asked.

I explained my situation. "I am just walking to take in the fresh air, I guess. There's nothing to do here for me because, as you can tell, I'm just a refugee. I sleep on a hungry stomach and wake up to continue the same cycle again. It's just survival."

A frown appeared on her face as she heard about my unfortunate circumstances. "That sounds rough! Are you sure you don't need any help?" she asked. Before allowing me to answer, she added, "If you're hungry, you should come over to my house. I'm just going back home. I'll make you tons of tasty food."

I went along with her. We got to her place, and she guided me inside and asked me to be seated. A man sat on the sofa. He appeared to be friendly and approachable.

"Oh, that is my boyfriend," she said, noticing my curiosity about the stranger. "We've been living together for quite a while now. You guys can be friends! It'll be comforting to have a new companion," Hasnaa said.

I politely agreed and smiled at the man.

Fikru, Alex, and Yohannes Meba, Place Menelik

Hasnaa went to the kitchen and began to chop vegetables for lunch. I started a conversation with the man. He was an interesting fellow, and though our mindsets didn't match and we didn't precisely click in that instant, he was friendly enough to keep the small talk going. Twenty minutes passed. Hasnaa chimed in on the conversation a few times from the kitchen.

After a couple more minutes, she came out all sweaty. She decorated the table with a feast. I ate until I felt full. I didn't talk at all while I ate. I just wanted to stuff my face.

Meeting Hasnaa at such an uncertain time of my life was genuinely a great experience. Yet again, I could clearly sense the hand of God at work in my life. Her house had a welcoming aura, and the people around her were friendly. She was also kind enough to purchase clothes for me and offer for me to visit her place as often as I liked. She promised to cook me meals whenever I didn't have enough food to get by and allowed me to stay comfortably at her place without worrying about being a nuisance.

I didn't know how I could reciprocate her kindness, and at that time, I barely had the resources to do so. But I made a promise to myself that I would eventually pay her back once I changed my current conditions. Receiving help like that ignited hope within me, reminding me that this place shouldn't be foreign to me anymore. At least I could turn to someone for guidance and comfort when I felt the weight of the world on my shoulders.

I was thrilled that I met Hasnaa. A few days after the interaction, I bumped into Daniel Memba, a guy I'd met during my daily walks, who I chatted with often. He was a talkative and outgoing person, someone who could befriend any stranger easily. I enjoyed talking to him. So that day, as usual, I went over to hang out with him.

We talked about the scorching weather of Djibouti and how abandoned the streets felt by 11:00 p.m. as barely anyone left their house late at night. The small talk continued till he brought up an offer that I just couldn't resist.

Daniel leaned against the wall and said, "I've been living in this small house with four other people. It doesn't have enough space, but the rent is distributed among us, so that saves me the money."

I replied without much thought, "I've been living in that roofless place for so long. It's insane. It's better than what I had before though. Ha-ha!"

Daniel looked at me strangely and said, "You've really been living there for so long?"

I laughed and looked at the ground.

He said, "I mean, we have enough space for another person to join us. Do you want to share the rent?"

I was taken aback by the sudden suggestion. I didn't need to give it much thought because I genuinely needed another place to stay. I was grateful to Alo for finding me a place to live for the time being, but living in a house sounded far better than tossing and turning in a roofless area.

I immediately accepted the offer and began living in that house the next day. It was much better having a proper mattress to sleep on along with a roof above my head. It wasn't difficult sharing the house with five other individuals; the only problem was the rent would eat up most of our expenses. We slept on empty stomachs to gather money for rent worth 10,000 franc monthly. Again, every day seemed like a fight for survival.

In the meantime, I decided to pursue an education in Cairo. I realized I needed to start somewhere. It would be near impossible to go to America after receiving my refugee card, so I had to select a reachable country. I applied for a scholarship to American University in Cairo and even took a test. I had no clue how many people had applied, nor did I consider myself accomplished enough to grasp the opportunity, but I took the chance anyway.

I passed the test and was among the five people who were selected. I was surprised once I received the notification since I was genuinely unsure of the outcome. This showed that God indeed was with me. My trust and faith in Him grew immensely with each passing day. I celebrated the achievement with my roommates. Apart from the day I got the refugee card, this was the most joyous day for me in Djibouti.

I spent the next few days feeling closer than ever to finalizing my journey and getting to the end point of it all. After this sponsorship, I would apply for the United States because I would have enough credibility by then. Afterward, I would bring over my family and, of course, Martha so they could taste the American dream too. I couldn't wait for our monochromatic life to blossom with dazzling colors.

I had received the visa, and every other formality in the way was catered to as well. I was truly leaving for a new country, legally this time; it felt surreal. The UNHCR was providing me with funds for my luggage, so I visited the agency to collect the money.

As I reached the reception desk and explained my situation, the man began to search for my file. He continued to do that for far too long, and I was scared he had lost my file. He fumbled through the files and documents spread on his desk and eventually lifted his head to explain the problem to me. "I'm sorry, but your file isn't here anymore. It was sent to the American embassy from what I'm seeing."

I blinked in confusion and couldn't speak for a minute or two. I leaned forward and exclaimed, "What?"

I stuttered, trying to find the right words, but I couldn't. I blew air out of my nose and took a deep breath to regain my senses. "What has happened? Why would they send it to the American embassy?"

It all felt like a lie and gave me goose bumps.

The man collected the papers and started to tidy them up. "The US government is providing a resettlement program for five thousand refugees in areas like Kenya, Djibouti, and Sudan to immigrate to the USA," he said, adjusting his glasses. "It appears that your file is selected with other refugees, and that's why your file has been sent to the embassy."

I forgot about Cairo or how I somehow got selected. I just dashed outside. I immediately ran toward the US embassy. I ran till I couldn't feel my legs anymore and till my knees felt weak. I forgot how much I wanted this opportunity. I never knew that my fate would possibly unfold like this, that the universe would come together to bring me a step closer to ending my journey successfully. It overwhelmed me, and I wanted to break down crying in the middle of the street, but I had to be a bit stronger ... just a little bit more.

I reached the embassy and pushed through the door. In a panicked state, I looked around to locate who I could talk to. My breath was uneven, and the soles of my feet hurt, but as the sudden news numbed me, I barely sensed the pain. I finally relaxed and figured I had to speak to the secretary sitting at the right of the entrance. I made my way toward her and asked about the issue.

She checked the system and the pile of files at the corner. She confirmed that my file was indeed placed there and told me that the number assigned to me was forty-seven. I was frazzled yet still sensible enough to ask for the interview details. I knew I had nothing to lose, and allowing this opportunity to pass by me would be one of my gravest mistakes ever. I went for the interview without batting an eye or mentally preparing myself. I walked into the room, answered questions for what felt like half an hour, and came out questioning whether I was stuck in a dream or not.

I was informed the results would be posted the next morning around ten o'clock. I thanked them for their services and left for home. On my way back, I had a constant smile on my face. There was a tingling feeling in the pit of my stomach. I had never felt so fulfilled. It was as if this was what I had been born to do, and now I had accomplished it. The feeling of every struggle and pain of mine turning into fruits eased my wounded heart. I was grateful to myself for not giving up during times of adversity and carrying on even when I felt powerless. I realized I was at long last seeing the results that I had risked my life for, and happiness overwhelmed me. I wanted to cry my eyes out but also laugh freely.

Once I arrived home, I didn't inform anyone about the interview. Everyone believed I simply went to collect my funds for Cairo and would leave in six days. But I wasn't going anymore. There wasn't a single cell in my body inclined toward leaving for Cairo; all I could think of was the interview and its results, which would come out tomorrow.

I woke up early in the morning and checked whether everyone around me was asleep. I slowly closed the door behind me so that I could leave without any questions asked. It wasn't that I didn't wish to inform these men about my accomplishment; I just didn't possess the energy to deal with the questions that they would surely bombard me with. They would ask why I was so easily ditching an actual opportunity in Cairo to leave for America, where my future would be blurry and unsure.

I desperately wanted to check the results and satisfy the suspense that tugged at me. I just hoped to see if I made it to the list. Every step that I took toward the embassy felt heavy. My heartbeat was thumping.

I reached the embassy at the perfect time because I could see a row of papers glued to the walls by the corner. They had names and numbers written on them in no specific order. I scanned through the entire collection, carefully checking each name. I kept staring at the list—till tears ran down my face.

I saw it. I saw my name and the number forty-seven written beside it.

That was the first time in years that I genuinely cried my eyes out. My entire face was wet with tears while I tried to catch my breath. I wiped my face and sighed loudly, tracing my thoughts back to what ignited this journey and how I was about to achieve my happy ending.

Even as I wanted to celebrate this moment, I felt emotional because of the unreal situation before me. I held my head in my hands and wailed till I let everything out. I cried because I knew I was finally out of the miserable loop my life had been in. I would now spend my old age in America and raise my children in a country where they could chase their dreams and strive for their ambitions without any restrictions.

I was at the stage where I thanked God for making me strong enough to withstand prison and humiliation. I thanked Him for helping me endure the trauma that had besieged me checkpoint after checkpoint. I cried for myself. In that sadness, I celebrated myself as well for coming out through every difficult situation, without ever letting it break me.

I wasn't a sturdy man, nor was I powerful enough to lift heavy objects, but I had an elastic heart that stretched to make room for people I loved. I was willing to lay down my own life to secure their future. If I had to do everything all over again, I wouldn't have wanted it any other way. Even in my family, I wasn't always the strongest or the most popular sibling, but who cared? I was about to set foot in a land that had felt oceans away. Now, as I gazed at the paper with my name on it, I realized that hard work did indeed pay off.

After seeing the results and knowing where I was set to travel, I decided I wasn't departing for Cairo anymore. Though my visa was already issued and every necessary preparation for my leave had been completed, I couldn't convince myself to go anymore. There wasn't a reason for me to go, so I went to the UN office to inform the counselor about my circumstances and change of mind.

Seid, Hasnaa's boyfriend, Daniel, and Fikru

Much to my surprise, she displayed shock and appeared somewhat offended by my words. She squinted at me and said in a condescending tone, "Who sent your file to the embassy?"

I was taken aback by her harsh tone, so I answered her with confusion. "It wasn't me, of course. I'm sorry, but I don't work here. It was an employee from here who delivered my file."

She wasn't convinced in the slightest, and her tone turned even more unfriendly. "You're unwilling to go to Cairo anymore after getting all the proceedings cleared. Don't you think that someone else could've gotten the opportunity instead of you? You took away the chance of two people!"

I stared at her. I understood her concern, and she was right, but I couldn't help it. I just couldn't leave for Cairo anymore. "If you don't pass the medical examination conducted by the embassy," the counselor began, "you won't be going anymore."

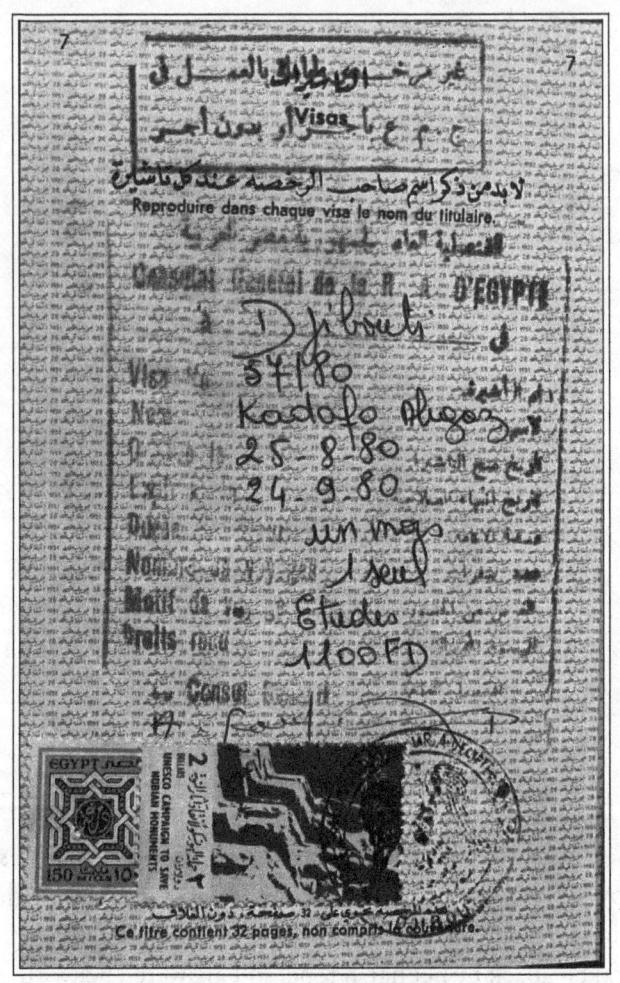

Egypt student visa (1980)

There was finality in her voice, and I knew she was powerful enough, as well as affiliated with the UN, to stop me from leaving altogether. I felt sick to my stomach because now I had another problem on my plate. Just when everything seemed to be aligned and my worries had subsided, I was greeted with this time bomb. There were twenty-one days until the results of the medical examination of the selected candidates that the embassy had conducted would be revealed. I was already panicking about the outcome.

When I came home from the UN office, I locked myself in the bathroom. I knelt on its cement floor and let my tears flow. While crying, I clasped my hands together and let out a prayer to God. He had helped me throughout this journey, bringing me to this destination while other people were fantasizing about getting here. I knelt and closed my bloodshot eyes, then let out a prayer to the *Lord:* "God, if You're out there, if You're listening, please hear my concern. If You can allow me to pass the medical exam and make it to America, I would give myself to You."

Fikru Aligaz (Djibouti, 1980)

I prayed so silently that it felt like I'd whispered the words to the wind so they could be carried somewhere far away. I kept muttering the prayer to myself, hoping my words would manifest as my reality. And I was astonished when they did! When I received the examination results, I found out that I had passed the test without any complications. That was when I knew without any doubt that God really existed.

My journey was filled with many twists and turns, and I suffered greatly at many points along the way, but the end result was beyond my greatest dreams. I understood that God was guiding me along the right path. He was helping me combat and overcome my miserable experiences—and to learn valuable lessons from them. The Lord had already set everything in place for my success, though at the time I did not realize it. Many times in life, there are things that happen to us that can only be viewed through the eyes of faith.

I departed for America on September 29, 1980, a day I will never forget for the rest of my life. Before leaving for the airport, I bade farewell to the people I was close to in Djibouti. We hugged it out and exchanged encouraging words. They wished me well on my new quest. I realized I was surrounded by great people. Alo and Hasnaa lent me a shoulder when I felt alone and scared. I made sure to express my gratitude to each one of them.

Leaving for America was a joyous moment for me, but that didn't mean I forgot I was living in a terrible place. With a grimace, I chillingly recalled a disturbing incident that had happened not long before my scheduled departure date. I always enjoyed my everyday walks around the city, but I had to be careful no matter which street I passed because the police were especially hard on the refugees.

They would arrest and toy with them on the streets just for the fun of it. If the police caught a refugee, they would be thrown into jail for three days, even if they didn't commit a crime and were just minding their own business. This discrimination against refugees scared me at first, but I decided I needed to adjust somehow. So, I walked on the streets whenever I wanted, though I stayed cautious at all times.

However, I wasn't as careful as I thought I was because the day I received my visa, I was put into jail by a police officer strolling around. I was out with my friend on one of our regular walks, and the officer grabbed us and threw us into jail simply because we were refugees.

In that instant, I realized I shouldn't be leaving my house at all. I couldn't be careful enough, no matter how much I tried. If I wanted to go to America, I needed to stay indoors. That's why I remained inside my house for many days till the day I had to depart for the airport.

I packed what little I had and reached the airport two hours earlier than the takeoff time. I couldn't fathom being even a minute late. I had a medium-sized bag and a water bottle to accompany me through the trip. Once I reached the airport and lined up for the checking process, I noticed police officers pulling selected people out of the lines.

It must've been because they appeared suspicious or didn't possess enough evidence to support their identities. I began to sweat as I underwent every formality required in the process. I couldn't even begin to think about what would happen if they pulled me aside. I was nervous as I stared at the police examining the people they were pulling out of line, but luckily enough, I boarded the plane.

The door closed behind me, and we were guided inside. I placed my luggage in the respective section and sat by the window. The plane lifted into the air after a wait of ten minutes. As I witnessed the distance between the ground and myself increase, I felt the heavy burden from my shoulders slowly disappearing. I leaned back, feeling lighter than ever.

I had made it.

CHAPTER 17

Coming to the United States

I glanced outside the window to see whether I was really on my way to America or not. I wanted to pinch my cheeks and slap myself hard to make sure that everything was in fact real. It all seemed like a fantasy, just a silly dream of mine somehow coming true. I stared at the puffy clouds that I was floating on and noticed how I was one with the sky.

I leaned back in my chair and let out a deep sigh. It wasn't a painful sigh or a tired one. It was a sigh of freedom from the shackles that had confined me. At that moment, I felt I could never feel so liberated in my entire life.

An hour passed before the plane finally landed. We were staying in France for a while and would then continue our journey to the States. Once I left the plane, I roamed around the shops and stores just to window-shop. My pockets were empty, so I knew I couldn't afford to purchase a souvenir for Martha or my family. Curiously, I picked up two items on display and stared at them. But then I saw small postcards tucked neatly on a stand.

They were beautiful, with colorful scenery painted on them. Instantly, I realized I should send Martha a postcard to inform her I would reach America in a few hours. I asked for a pen from an employee and scribbled away. Among other things, I wrote *I kept my promise to you. I'm heading to America now.*

These were simple words that wouldn't possess much meaning for a stranger who had never walked in my shoes. But I knew how gut-wrenchingly hard it had been to fulfill that promise and even step foot in a foreign land. I knew what it felt like to stare death and fear in the face and still make it out alive.

I dropped the postcard in a nearby mailbox and boarded the plane, as the operator announced we would depart for New York soon. After seven to eight hours of flight, I arrived in New York, and it felt very long. My heart was frantically beating in my chest, and my nervousness spiked. It wasn't that I was unsure how I would begin my life in a new land or if I had the means to survive. It was merely the fact that a lifelong dream of mine was finally coming true before my very eyes. The thought itself was sending chills down my spine.

Finally, I had reached America! I turned my head in different directions to take in my surroundings. I saw busy passengers running to greet their families, tourists strolling around the airport with maps clutched in their hands, and children tugging at their parents to get them candies from nearby vendors.

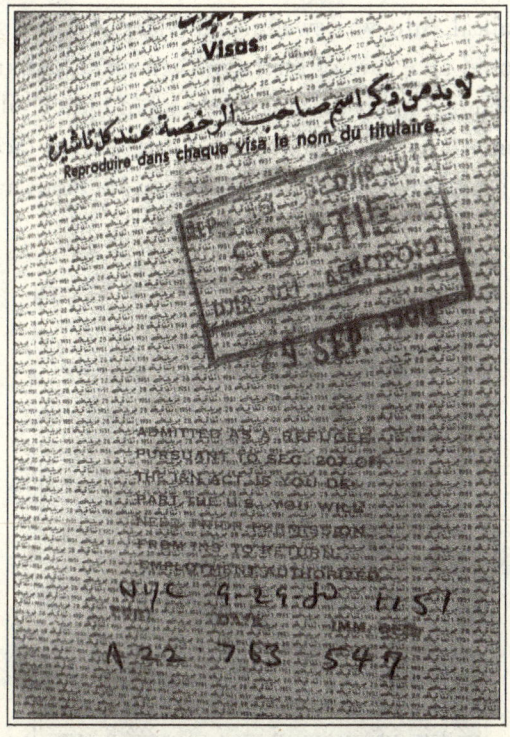

Visa, admitted as a refugee, September 29, 1980

There were around forty to forty-five refugees along with me, all of whom came from Djibouti. I saw plenty of them change their routes and go to different states than the one I was planning for. I was supposed to leave for Washington, DC, so I needed to board the plane again after taking a short break. Every refugee had a person waiting for them at the entrance to guide them and issue immigration. I greeted the man, who mentioned he would help with the paperwork so I could depart for Washington smoothly.

I reached Washington after a quick flight. I was happy to finally land in the city, but I just couldn't bring myself to display that excitement. My head felt like it could burst open, as if there was a tight plastic band wrapped around it. My eyes were droopy, and my body was weaker than ever. I figured I was jet-lagged after spending so many hours sitting on planes and changing time zones, and I just couldn't shrug away the pain and exhaustion.

Finally, I saw someone standing up and waving at me. I identified that person as my sister, Turuwork Aligaz, who lived in Arlington, Virginia, with her children, Raheal, Adnew, Zewedu, and Nigest. She was supposedly my sponsor and would take care of me from then on. I had known I would meet her once I landed in my designated area, but I just couldn't hold back my tears. It seemed it had been years since I had seen her face or interacted with her. I had forgotten how she looked and was nervous making my way toward her.

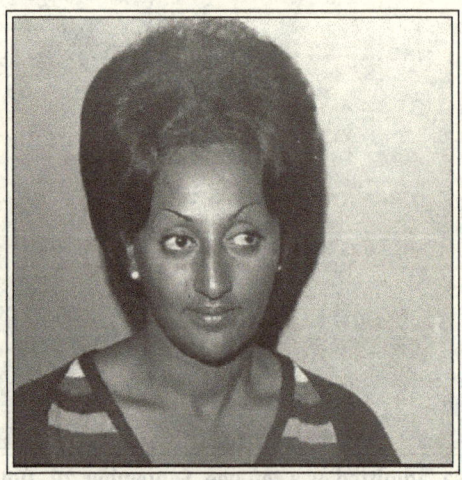

The late Ms. Turuwork Aligaz

As I closed the distance between us, she extended her arms and embraced me. I immediately collapsed in her embrace and let my tears flow. She wiped away my tears and stared at me lovingly. She didn't ask any questions and simply allowed me to take a step back and collect myself. I would be living with her, so she could leave the questioning and small talk for later.

I got to my sister's place and talked to her for half an hour before going to bed. I told her about my life in Djibouti and what led me to leave Ethiopia and how often I had to deal with the authorities. I talked about the terrible situation of the country I fled and why I needed to bring my fiancée, Martha, and family here as soon as possible.

She listened to me silently, allowing me to pour my heart out. Everything was so emotional for me, and I was undeniably overwhelmed as I began to share my experiences. It reminded me how awful and cruel everything I went through was, and it shocked me how I had bounced back from that misery.

It felt great just to let my thoughts out, but I couldn't continue to talk for long because my head was throbbing with pain. I went to bed and slept through the night and woke up at midnight the next day. I wanted to keep sleeping, but I also needed to eat. My sister prepared a huge meal for me, which I devoured as soon as I woke up. Again, after eating, I went back to sleep and woke up at irregular hours. I couldn't continue to sleep because I needed to sort my luggage and find a job and settle in.

My sister helped me collect the necessary documents and got them cleared in a week or two so that I could find a job. Thanks to her, I snagged a busboy job at a nearby restaurant.

The experience of working as a busboy was enlightening. It was fun learning the basics of working in a restaurant and greeting people. Besides, I had to start somewhere. I also had some old friends of mine living forty miles away from my sister's apartment, where I was living. I would regularly meet and hang out with them to relieve stress and just have a great time. My life was flowing pretty well and had settled the way I wanted it to.

I had a job, and my income was enough to fulfill my needs while also allowing me to save for future plans. I was slowly but surely collecting money to secure myself in Washington without having to rely on my sister.

I was reminded that God was with me once again when, two months after my arrival, I met a strange man at the bus station. I was standing at the bus station, waiting to board the bus and leave for home. I was immersed in my own world and stared at the swaying trees before me when I noticed a gentleman standing right beside me.

He stared at me with a friendly smile. Considering how complex my life was till I reached this country, and how I was still living illegally as a refugee here, the experience with the unfamiliar man didn't sit well with me. I couldn't put my finger on why he was intently staring at me and leaning forward to start a conversation.

His pale skin looked paler under the sunlight, and his blue eyes were fixed on me. I stood awkwardly till the man broke the ice.

"Hi! It's quite sunny, isn't it?" he began, trying to start a conversation. I smiled at him in agreement. He stood shoulder to shoulder with me as if we were friends already. We talked about general things and boring everyday topics till he asked me, "So, where are you from?"

He noticed from my accent that I wasn't a born American and probably emigrated here from a foreign country. I won't lie; I was hesitant to answer that question because I didn't know what it could lead to. But I had already talked to the man, and he appeared reliable and unsuspicious. We boarded the bus and kept talking throughout the ride. I told him about my origins. "I came from Djibouti actually, but I'm originally from Ethiopia. I have settled here as a refugee."

His eyes widened in shock, but it wasn't as if the fact that I was a refugee disgusted him; if anything, he was now more interested in my journey. So, I began to explain my experiences to him but didn't dive too deep into the details. He listened intently until it was his turn to leave the bus. He glanced back at me, giving me a kind smile. "I need to get off now. My name is Christian Nagel (CB). Here, you can have my card to keep in touch." He handed me his business card and left the bus.

I carefully placed the card in my front pocket and forgot about it. As I got home and settled on the sofa, I told my sister about my new acquaintance, but she seemed skeptical about it all. It didn't seem natural for a stranger to stare at someone and start a conversation. She asked me to be as careful as I could be because you never know about the world, and I agreed with her.

Two weeks later, I was doing the laundry when I bent down to pick up a basket from the floor. Just as I lifted my head, I saw a card fall to the ground from my pocket. I paid it no mind till I saw a cross over it. I skimmed through the details, which left my mouth agape. The man I had met on the bus could help me in availing myself of sponsorship for Martha since he was associated with a religious organization. He appeared to be a minister of some sort and worked for an organization that could sponsor people for educational purposes. I couldn't let this opportunity slide by me. I already knew Christian Nagel (CB) anyway, so I believed it would be easy for me to convince him to help me.

I called him as soon as I could. The phone rang for a while before he eventually picked it up. "Hello! Who am I speaking to?"

"This is Kadafo speaking, the person you met at the bus station," I replied, keeping my tone friendly.

His voice immediately perked up. "Oh, yes! I was waiting to hear from you. How's it going?"

"It's the usual," I said. "Just running some errands and coming home for a nap."

He chuckled and said, "Well, it looks like you called because you saw my card and wanted to discuss business with me, I believe? Do you want to meet soon?"

"I can't for the moment … I … I have to go to DMV and get my driver's license."

He said, "If it's OK, you can use my car to get your license. We can also have a discussion afterward?"

As the message hit my ears, I was shocked. I couldn't believe he was willing to provide me his own car for a road test. It would be a big help, so I immediately agreed to his offer. However, my sister was quick to remind me of stranger danger and convinced me I should at least bring this man to her apartment so she could judge for herself.

The next day, I called him over just to ease my sister's suspicions. It was a rainy morning and quite windy outside, but he still came all the way up to our front door, standing outside with a dripping umbrella. My sister opened the door, and instead of allowing him to enter, she talked with him right outside the door before letting him enter. She checked his character, attire, and overall personality and eventually shot a smile his way. Finally, she allowed me to go with him, and we were on our way to the driving test.

CB was friendly all through the drive, joking around from time to time. I eventually got my license, using his car. I passed the road test quite easily. We later went to a nearby restaurant to grab some lunch around noon.

He placed his beige coat on the top of the chair beside him and adjusted his sleeves to prepare to dig into the food. "How's it all going? You said you came here as a refugee, right? What was all that like?" he asked, grabbing the menu on the side and skimming through it.

I let out a deep breath because, again, I was unsure where to begin. I started from the very beginning and explained every situation I had faced. I didn't sugarcoat or skip anything. I made sure he got to know the horrific ordeal I had been through. He listened to me with horror and shock in his eyes.

His hands that once rested casually on the restaurant menu twitched anxiously. Every word that left my mouth seemed to be a blow to his chest. He couldn't believe that a person might go through such harsh situations and yet switch their fate to benefit them.

After I told my story to him, he told me a bit about his background. "I'm a campus crusade minister," he said, while his fingers tapped on the table. "I go from campus to campus and help college students to know God and accept the Lord as their personal Savior."

He lifted his gaze to meet mine. "Would you be interested in accepting the Lord as your personal Savior?"

That question struck me, and it brought a wave of memories back. It reminded me of the time I had crouched on the bathroom floor and wept for my misery to subside. It was when I was desperate for clearing the medical examination and moving to America. I prayed too intently that day, almost as if I believed God was right beside me, and I was conversing with Him as if He were an old friend. I still remembered the words I whispered during the prayer: "If You take me out of this situation, I will give myself to You."

I replied to the man with conviction, "Yes, I can accept Him."

He noticed my eyes beaming with dedication. I was convinced God was the answer, and I was ready to dedicate my entirety to Him only. The man nodded. "Very well. Next week, I'll introduce you to a friend of mine, Steve. He will assist you further. In the meantime, I'll give you some Bible tracts to get the gist of everything."

He handed me a few tracts. I read through them while we ate our lunch. Eventually, I left with him in his car, as he agreed to drive me back home even though I insisted I was all right returning by myself. I appreciated his kindness.

The following week, I met CB at a McDonald's near Glebe Road / Columbia Pike, in Arlington, Virginia, where he sat with Steve Galebach and Craig Stern. They sat beside each other with a wide smile and straight posture, as if they were ready to discuss business at any time. Once I got seated, Steve asked me the same question. He wanted to know about my story. Again, I began to detail my past, ranging from the positive experiences to the days I rotted away in prison.

The man seemed amazed and shocked. His mouth was left open as I kept describing what I went through. It wasn't a great feeling to be going into such profound detail about experiences I didn't want to remember. Thankfully, the conversation switched to him, and he began to tell me about his own background. He told me he was a lawyer and appointed as the person who would take me to church every Wednesday and Sunday. The man explained, "I need to appoint Steve because he lives closer to where you live. I live in a different part of the town. So, it would be easier if he helped you."

I had no problem with it. I trusted CB enough to place a reliable person to supervise me. I didn't doubt his decision. I was ready to begin my quest in church and grow closer to God.

Of course, when I accepted the Lord as my Savior, I called my older brother, Hanfere, in Ethiopia, who himself was already a devout Christian believer. He was thrilled to hear that I had dedicated my life to Jesus.

And this was how my journey toward connecting with God and practicing religious values began. It was very interesting and exciting. My father was always a religious man, while I had a religious awakening after spending months on the road. I enjoyed speaking to God and following His Word. It reminded me I wasn't alone in this world, and no matter what hardship I might have to face, I was still protected by a higher being capable of pulling me out of my mess.

Every week, Steve would pick me up from my house, and we would leave for the church on the appointed day. During this time, I decided to move away from my sister's apartment and rent out a place of my own with my friend from Djibouti, Daniel Meba. I had saved up enough money to do so. Once I got my apartment and settled in, my regular visits to church were steady, and I was more than satisfied because it was my first time paying bills in general, and I was able to do that independently. Everything had fallen into place. Every puzzle piece that I had a hard time figuring out just fell right into the correct place, completing the picture. Those were truly some of the greatest days I had spent in my life altogether.

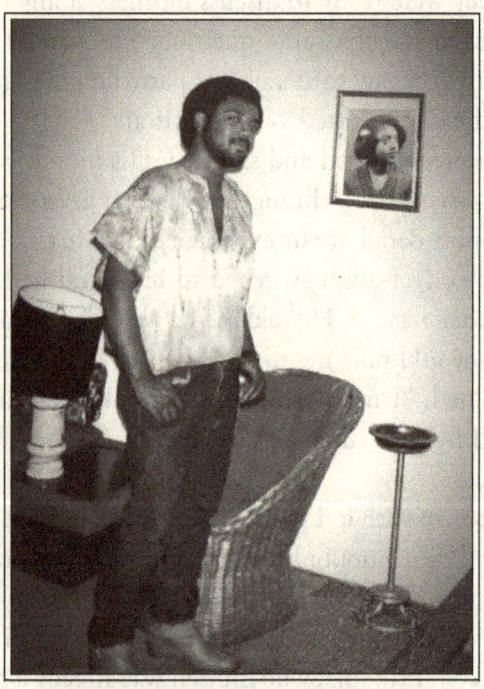

Fikru waiting for the love of his life

However, I was still worried about Martha and hoped to bring her here as quickly as I could. I remembered her patient smile and twinkling eyes. I wanted to hug her and take her out of the mess she was stuck in. A month or two passed. I thought it was about time that I talked to Steve about my fiancée and the entire sponsorship procedure.

On a Sunday, when we were supposed to spend another regular day at church, I brought up the topic. I told him how I wished to bring Martha here and asked if he could sponsor her. He didn't dismiss my idea and, to the contrary, showed interest in it.

A week passed, and as he dropped me off at church, he handed me an envelope. I stared at it, confused for a second, but my heart began to race when I remembered how I had asked for the sponsorship days ago. He gave me the envelope and tapped my shoulder as if to say, "I got you." Once I opened the envelope, I was overwhelmed. I felt tears pooling in my eyes and an immense lump in my throat.

I found the sponsor affidavit support and school fee that he had already paid. Everything was done and completed with no hassles. There wasn't a single thing I needed to do; all I had to do was just talk to Martha and prepare for her to come here.

The following night, I called Martha and told her about the package and formalities that Steve had completed for me. Her voice was cheery and light. It filled the hole inside my chest, dug through months of despair. I forgot how much I'd missed hearing her voice and her little laughs in between conversations.

"I have everything, Martha," I said to her.

She gasped and laughed at the same time. "You really did it. I can't believe it!" she cried.

I could tell from her voice that she was proud of me and couldn't wait to meet me again. I felt the same.

"Don't be too late! You have to settle the procedures there too," I said, trying to make everything simple for her. "You don't have to take the burden of it all on yourself. You should meet my brother. I think you know the one I'm talking about. He will help you with the passport."

She sounded confused, so I reassured her. "It's OK. I know you'll do this. Stay strong for both of us!"

Just like that, our phone call ended, and I crouched to the ground, silently praying in my heart that everything would go well. I didn't want to deal with any complications anymore. I didn't want any pit stops or red signs at this point. Everything needed to flow perfectly because I couldn't afford to lose the one chance I had of bringing Martha into this country. Though I could always find another sponsor, I still wanted Martha to reach America with the first sponsor I found because who knew when I could bag another one.

My worries subsided when I found out that Martha had received her passport. The other procedures involved took plenty of time, however. It took six months for Martha to get clearance and finally board the plane to depart for America. During that time, my roommate, Daniel Meba, decided to move to Dallas, Texas, and I was alone until my brother and his children came to stay with me.

On the day of Martha's arrival, we went to the airport to collect her. I was more of a nervous mess than anyone there. I just couldn't sit or stand still because I feared what Martha would be subjected to. What if they stopped her from entering? I couldn't comprehend such a horrific possibility. I anxiously waited outside the airport. Steve went along with us as a source of support if things got out of hand. Luckily, Martha entered the country.

I still remember the way her face lit up once she saw me waiting for her. She was so joyous, and we embraced, laughing and crying into each other's arms. It felt like forever since Martha's scent surrounded me, and I hugged her petite body. I hoped for this moment to continue forever and for us to stay happy for the coming years in America.

She was angry at me for hiding the actual process I followed to reach this country. I didn't have any American men involved to help me safely come to this country as I had told her before. After I left for my journey, she began to ask the surrounding people. She figured I left as a refugee and was continuing a rather dangerous path. I could never tell her I was leaving illegally as a refugee because I knew she would worry too much, like always.

She would have tried to stop me from beginning the journey altogether and would have asked me to stay home. I didn't have another option, so I needed to hide the truth from her. It was the only thing I ever hid from Martha, and seeing how hurt she was from my lie, I promised myself to never lie to her again.

I took Martha to my sister's apartment, where she sat down with my nephew and niece. We all had a wonderful time together. My sides hurt from the constant giggles and fits of laughter. I was happy and living in the moment—a sensation I believed I was forgetting. My life seemed to be back on track.

Considering that we had been apart for so many years, we noticed how our personalities had changed, especially mine. Martha was surprised to see the changes in me and that I had devoted myself to God. I was a

Christian man who lived and dedicated the entirety of his time to the Lord, which helped me quit my bad habits.

Martha was always encouraging me to participate in some kind of sport because she was an athletic woman, exceptional at volleyball especially, so she emphasized the importance of a healthy body and mind. As she saw me resorting to healthy habits and trying to take care of myself, she was surprised and tremendously happy for me.

Before we got married, Steve introduced us to the Rev. Richard A. Lord, assistant rector at the Church of the Apostles Episcopal in Fairfax, Virginia, and scheduled a marriage counseling session. After the session finished, we completed a water baptism class, and we both got baptized. Steve was there to witness our baptism. What a great moment to see your dream as it unfolds in this fashion! What a great moment to see yourself getting baptized with your fiancée at the same time. It was indeed a dream-come-true moment for me. Now that I had become a full-fledged Christian, Martha also accepted the Lord and began attending church with me.

With Steve's help, we planned to hold our wedding at the Church of the Apostles' main sanctuary in Fairfax, Virginia. The Rev. Richard A. Lord, assistant rector, agreed to officiate the wedding ceremony, including Holy Communion. I remember waking up around six thirty on that cold morning of January 9, 1982, without an alarm clock, waiting to for my big day to begin. I don't recall having any anxiety or tension, but I do remember getting ready and being thrilled to finally say, "I do," and become Martha's husband.

My best man, Steve, and nephew Jonny and Fikru

The wedding party finally arrived at the church at around 12:30 p.m. I know the ceremony would not start until two o'clock. At around one o'clock, my brother came to visit me in the dressing room to see how I was doing, which, of course, was a perfect moment for just the two of us. We anxiously hung out in that little room, peering out the window because we had a bird's-eye view of all the guests arriving, which was fun.

**My brother, Hanfere Aligaz, walked
Martha down the aisle**

After that, the wedding ceremony started, and following the officiating pastor, my best man and I entered from the side of the church and took our places at the altar. Then the groomsmen and the bridesmaids walked down the aisle in pairs and took their places as well. Martha, the bride, was escorted down the aisle by my brother, who stood on her left side, and together, they proceeded down the hall toward me. I turned around and took a step forward to greet my bride. Martha took her place next to me, standing on my left. After my brother, Hanfere Aligaz, gave her away, he took his seat next to his wife, Yeti Haile, in the first row.

REFUGEE & HOPE

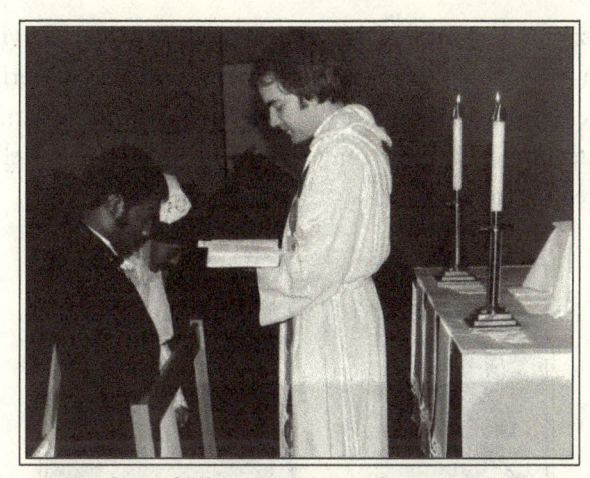

Martha and Fikru receiving Holy Communion, conducted by the Rev. Richard A. Lord

Taking our sacred vows, Martha and I tied the knot on that cold afternoon on January 9, 1982, a day that I could never forget in my entire life for two reasons. In traditional weddings, the bride's father walks her down the aisle and gives her away. In this case, my brother, whom I considered my role model, gave Martha away, which made it so special. On the other hand, Steve was my best man, and he played a vital role in sponsoring Martha and handling the wedding ceremony in the church. When I look back over my life, Steve was why my dream became a reality, and Martha and I are forever indebted to him for his kindness and the true Christlike love he has shown to us.

The wedding cake with the flower girl, my niece, Lili Hanfere

I felt fuzzy and warm from the inside because I was marrying the love of my life in America. I had fulfilled my promise and was greeting my wife in her gorgeous white dress, which complemented her beautiful, tanned skin. At that moment, I raised my closed fist to the sky to tell the world that I had really made it.

Mrs. and Mr. Aligaz

Elena, Jonny, Fikru, Martha, and Lili

Martha and Fikru enjoying each other

Moreover, it was at about this same time that my brother, Hanfere Aligaz, felt called to start the first Ethiopian church here in Washington, DC. I introduced my brother to Steve Galebach, and together they helped establish the first Ethiopian church in 1983. I still declare it to be one of my greatest blessings. Our church ended up having close to sixty to seventy people in a short time.

When I think back to how this all came about, I recall those early day when I was just settling in this country. I used to visit the back of a restaurant along with five other people, and we started our own home church. That number steadily grew to fifteen. Today, the International Ethiopian Evangelical Church of Washington, DC, has over one thousand members. Words cannot adequately express how proud I am of everyone who lent us a hand in forming the church and making my brother's vision a reality.

I knew that I wouldn't be anywhere without the help of the people in my life. They not only guided me but also stayed by my side to support my decision to spread the Lord's Word. The small community of only two people grew to become something wonderful, something that I couldn't help but feel proud of, though of course all of the credit and glory belongs to God Almighty, through whom all good things come.

CHAPTER 18

Life Continues

As our church grew, Martha became the first International Ethiopian Evangelical Church choir member and encouraged me to join the choir as well. Later, in 1984, I joined the choir and continued to sing acapella because there was no accompanist in the church. I traveled to Chicago to attend the annual conference of the Ethiopian Evangelical Churches Fellowship in North America. I saw the famous and prominent gospel singer Addisu Werku play the keyboards and sing. I felt goose bumps. Immediately after the session, my desire to play the keyboard was so strong that I asked brother Addisu Werku how to play the keyboard, and he advised me to buy one and learn it myself. Soon after, I bought a Casio keyboard and started playing songs, but things didn't go very well at first. However, after a lengthy period of trial and error, thank goodness, I learned a song or two and was able to accompany the choir.

First choir of IEEC

Fikru's first keyboard

The desire to serve the Lord became increasingly apparent from that day, and Martha and I decided to go to college, though we did not know where. After prayer and discussion, we both felt that we wanted to pursue our education and get our degrees while we were at it, and we were encouraged in this endeavor by my mentor, Dr. Melese Wegu, who suggested several universities. We eventually moved to Olathe, Kansas, but when we first arrived, we had no place to live there. Thankfully, our dear friends Atalfim and Dr. Solomon Bekele welcomed us to their home, and we stayed with them until we found an apartment of our own. We then began attending MidAmerica Nazarene University.

Martha and Fikru, Olathe, Kansas

Martha was studying Christian education and counseling, while I went for church music. We were both working and continuing our education. Some people might consider this lifestyle to be tough or stressful, but it was nothing compared to what led me to this place. I didn't necessarily enjoy yawning early in the morning and leaving for work, especially in winters, but having Martha by my side kept me motivated.

Martha and Fikru, college photo

We were finally together, living under the same roof. The past felt like a distant dream, but I never tried to push it all away. Living happily with Martha was a possibility that my dreadful journey helped me to accomplish. God had something precious in store for me. He knew I was capable of struggling from the bonds that society had wrapped me with and wiggling out.

My wife began to work at a Honeywell, while I took a part-time job at Johnson County Community College. Then the year 1988 rolled in, and I was offered a full-time position at my workplace and worked the entire night. I juggled my education and job.

Every day was a hustle. I would take out some crisp, ironed shirts and clean, dark shoes and leave for work. My wife did the same. Sometimes we came home too tired to even communicate. I would just lie down on the couch, feeling sluggish and fatigued, hoping to catch a wink of sleep. Even though Martha would be tired and heaving a sigh, she still prepared warm meals or brought me a cup of tea or coffee.

Martha Aligaz

She did more for me than I could ever have imagined. Her loving words were enough to heal my soul from the inside out. The consistent wide smile on her face made my heart flip. We had been married for a while now, but we behaved like a newlywed couple, dressing up for weekend dates and giving each other romantic surprises.

Martha and Fikru with traditional Ethiopian clothes

In 1988, Martha and I bought our first house. It wasn't extraordinary or lavish per se, just a typical, cozy house you would find anywhere in Olathe, Kansas. Still, we purchased a home by saving up enough through our sheer hard work and willpower. We saved up bit by bit like a bird collecting water droplets to extinguish a scorching fire. I firmly believe that staying dedicated can change anyone's life. I persevered and hoped, despite having been locked up several times and having stared death in the face more often than I care to remember. Staying balanced when confronted by such great misery is a true talent.

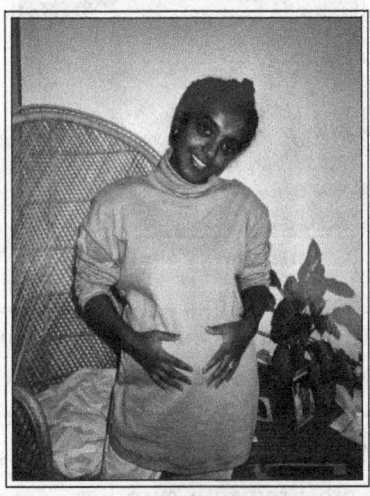

Martha's pregnancy with our first child

In the year 1990, we finished college, which was a great feat, something I remember clearly to this day. However, this wasn't the only life-changing news we received that year. Martha told me she was pregnant! Her eyes were pooling with tears, but she was smiling wide. I pulled her into a long, warm hug after the news, resisting tears of happiness.

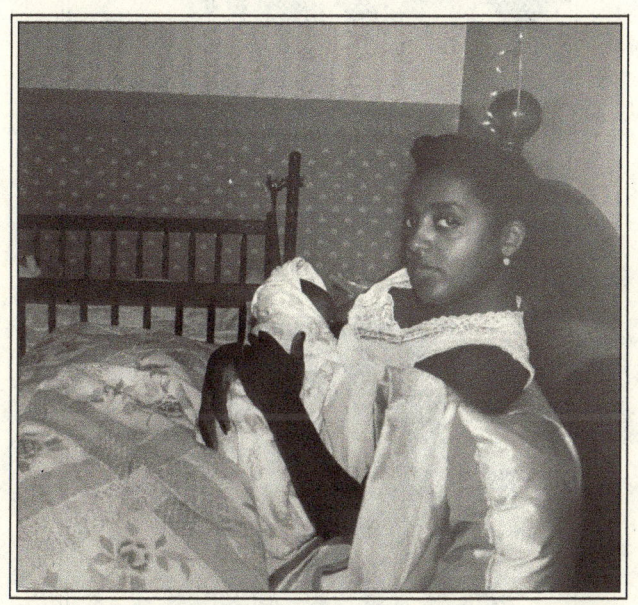

Martha holding Lydia after giving birth on August 14, 1990

Finally, praise to the Lord, an angel came down from heaven. After a nine-month journey, with our love for God increasing by the day, we were blessed with a baby girl. My wife and I were happy and grateful to have the beloved girl God had given us. Being the father of a beautiful girl for the first time was the happiest day of my life, and I was thrilled to be able to hug my daughter for the first time.

We all agree that having children is one of the sweetest blessings the Lord has given us. They are a constant reminder of His kindness and love for each of us. As our firstborn, Lydia has brought lots of happiness and joy into our family. "For we are God's handiwork, created in Christ Jesus to do good works, which God prepared in advance for us to do."

Martha and Lydia

My mother holding Lydia

I was busy with schoolwork, but that doesn't mean I forgot about God's call. The desire to find a place of worship for the Ethiopian Christian

Fellowship Church was still strong within me. When we came to Kansas, the one thing I noticed was that there weren't any formal churches except a weekly Bible study group held at Mrs. Atalefim and Dr. Solomon's home and others.

Martha and I became a part of this home church comprised of only a handful of people. We met people from all walks of life there, including Dr. Aschalew Kebede, who at the time was studying for his PhD at the University of Missouri, and visited every Friday for Bible study, prayer, fellowship, and spreading the Word of God. He was a dear brother with a humble attitude and always helped us out whenever he could. After our host family, Atalfim and Dr. Solomon Bekele, left Olathe, Kansas, for good, moving to South Carolina, Dr. Aschalew Kebede and others led this home church.

That was when the talk of establishing the first Ethiopian Christian Fellowship Church in Kansas came into play. There were eight to ten people visiting the group, but with our efforts and resilience, the numbers grew significantly. It didn't occur overnight. It took numerous visits and spreading the word around the neighborhood to inform people.

Those eight people grew till we had more than thirty people in our group, and the number just continued to grow exponentially. My dedication and hard work for the church helped it grow from a home church to the first Ethiopian Christian Fellowship Church in Kansas. Again, I had made my mark and spread God's influence in yet another place.

I was incredibly blessed and proud of myself for assisting Dr. Aschalew Kebede and others in finding a worship place at Assembly of God Church, 920 West Spruce Street, Olathe, Kansas, the first Ethiopian church in the state. I knew I was simply fulfilling God's will. He helped me during the times I felt like collapsing. He stood before me and always consoled me. Now, it was my turn to use my God-given gifts to honor God, and I knew this was the Lord's calling for me. "Sacrifice thank offerings to God, fulfill your vows to the Most High, and call on me in the day of trouble; I will deliver you, and you will honor me" (Psalm 50:14–15 New International Version).

This all occurred when Martha was six months pregnant with our first daughter. Also at this time, I was promoted to a leadership position in my job. I couldn't believe that my life was flowing so smoothly. I would lie awake at night and just think of how blessed I was to live a life devoted to a proper cause and have a loving wife.

I made a promise to myself that I would work hard for my family and devote my life to them. I would make sure my children received a good education. I would be a loving father so they would know they could share even their deepest secrets with me. It was also around this time that I started to figure out my true vision.

I wanted to start a music ministry. After spending months in churches and earning a degree in church music, I believed the music ministry reflected me the best, and I wanted to spread my passion for it to people searching for the Lord. My love for the music ministry was sparked when I was attending a New Year's program at the Ethiopian Christian Fellowship Church in Houston, Texas. At that time, I had a vision about leading a mass choir. I knew in that instant God was asking me to pursue this journey.

After much prayer and consulting with my wife and friends, the Bethel Music Ministry was founded formally in 1992. I named it Bethel Music Ministry based on a beautiful verse of scripture: "And let's arise and go up to Bethel, and I will make an altar there to God, who answered me on the day of my distress and has been with me wherever I have gone" (Genesis 35:3).

During that period, I traveled extensively all over America, at the invitation of local churches, to train their choirs and assist with revival conferences. In the process, I was able to recruit choir members who would join Bethel Music Ministry. At first, it seemed like an impossible task, but by the grace of God, I never became discouraged. It took me a bit longer than I'd initially anticipated to achieve my goal, but I knew it would become a reality, as God had promised everything—and He always delivers on His promises!

Bethel Praise and Worship Choir

After a long gestation period, in 1998, more than thirty men and women from different parts of the state and various walks of life came together to form the Bethel Praise and Worship Choir. One thing we all share is the Lord Jesus Christ and how He continues to impact our lives and the lives of the people to whom we minister. Since then, the choir has traveled twice a year to multiple locations throughout the US, including Atlanta, Georgia; Columbus, Ohio; Dallas, Texas; Denver, Colorado; Houston, Texas; Olathe, Kansas; Los Angeles, California; Minneapolis, Minnesota; Phoenix, Arizona; Seattle, Washington; and Washington, DC, as well as and Rome, Italy.

Bethel Praise and Worship Choir

It is the intention of this ministry to reach out to worshipers in the church who seek the intimacy of the secret place with the Father. Our ministry is also committed to helping people have their ailing bodies touched by God's healing, their troubled minds renewed, and their broken hearts mended.

No matter the size of the congregation, it is our desire to bring a fresh and positive approach. Just as the ancient Levites, priests, and musicians led the Israelites into battle with songs of praise and worship, a new generation is discovering the power of a broken and contrite heart, lifted up to God in profound expressions of love and adoration.

Each of the four living creatures had six wings and was covered with eyes all around, even under its wings. Day and night, they never stop saying: "Holy, holy, holy is the Lord God Almighty, who was, and is, and is to come." Whenever the living creatures give glory, honor and thanks to him who sits on the throne and who lives for ever and ever, the twenty-four elders fall down before him who sits on the throne and worship him who lives for ever and ever. They lay their crowns before the throne and say: "You are worthy, our Lord and God, to receive glory and honor and power, for you created all things, and by your will they were created and have their being." (Revelation 4:8–11 NIV)

The very first praise and worship service that I conducted in 1998 was a resounding success. It went so well in fact that one person accepted the Lord as their personal Savior. But I didn't achieve these results without struggle; that program drained the life out of me.

Bethel Praise and Worship Choir

About thirty-six of those people who volunteered showed up, which was unbelievable. I wasn't expecting so many to visit, as I thought they might be double minded about traveling far from home. However, a huge percentage of them showed up. I was forever grateful. We got our own hotel, catered our own meals, and took care of everything. There were also many outsiders skeptical of my success. They were convinced the ministry wouldn't last long and advised me to consider different options. But I kept my faith.

Throughout that time, I was constantly traveling on weekends from one city to another. I went back home on weekdays to work full-time and take care of my family. We had immense rehearsals and morning and night services on Sunday. I was exhausted when I got home. I believe I was extremely burnt out during that time, but this program was a good opportunity given to me by the Lord. It was a door He had opened for me to guide me to a path He believed would benefit me for years to come. And it truly did.

Martha holding Sharon with Fikru

God's plan for Martha and me was different from ours when we first got married. We tried for eight years before having our first child, and then another ten years passed before Martha was pregnant with our second daughter, Sharon, at the age of thirty-nine. We were so overwhelmed with the joy Sharon brought to our family. She, of course, was a blessing, and our lives will never be the same!

"These children will change our lives for the better," my wife had said, placing a comforting hand on her bulging belly.

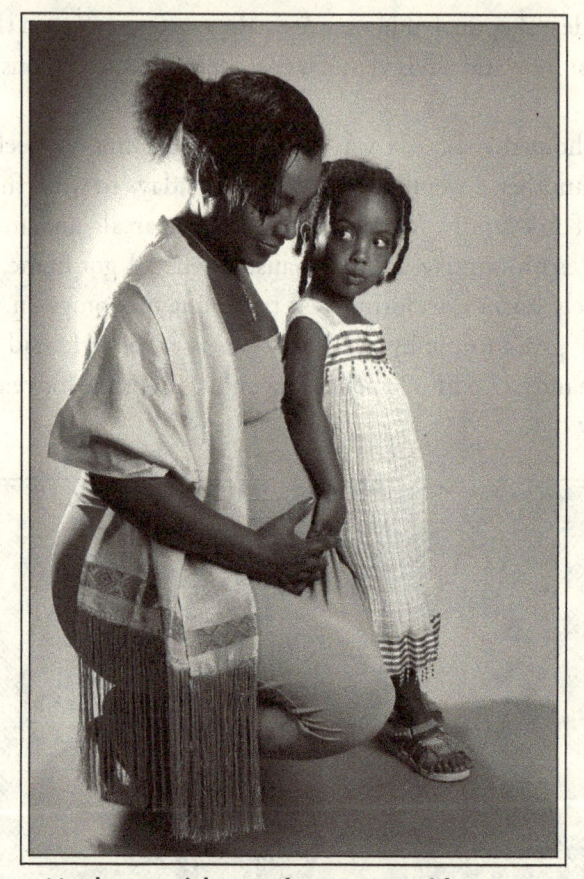

Martha was eight months pregnant with our son Emmanuel, and Sharon was standing next to her

She was pregnant with our son at that time. I nodded, grasping her hand tightly.

"You know, I prayed for you every day when I was in Ethiopia. Even after you reached America, I was just so nervous," she said.

I lowered my gaze and pursed my lips. "Me too. I was always thinking about you. I always dreamt about us starting a family. All of this seems like a dream." I sighed.

She got up and gave me a hug. I still remember the calm yet cheery look in her eyes, as if nothing could ever go wrong in life. Her jet-black hair was twisted into braids, and her doe eyes lovingly stared at her stomach.

Martha holding Emmanuel

"I will try my best to support you all," I whispered to myself. Having a baby is always a blessing, but you see, Emmanuel was more of a gift than you can imagine. It was a miracle! At that time, my wife and I were more than happy that our second daughter, Sharon, brought us so much happiness ten years after our firstborn daughter, Lydia. However, God did not finish His work, and an unexpected and very long-awaited miracle happened, and my wife gave birth to this little miracle at age forty-one. A complete family of five!

Fikru holding Sharon and Emmanuel

We had busy, packed schedules every day. Martha took a break in between her pregnancies, but she returned to work just as her health recovered. Our lives flowed smoothly with work, children, and love—the balance we had longed for, for so many years.

The ministry I established was touching many lives, and it was surreal to imagine I was capable of such a deed. The one thing that I loved dearly about my ministry was that all of us were joined at the hip. Most of the members belonged to different cities or states, but they loved one another beyond any limits. They were so strongly connected that spending a day without the other in the ministry felt strange and empty. We all call, text, and email whenever we can. The ministry had intense rehearsals and practice, and we chose set lists at night, yet no one complained, as we enjoyed staying together.

Now, the ministry has visited numerous states all over America for twenty-one years, spreading the love of God. As the community continued to grow, we influenced more than a hundred people to accept the Lord. These people were from all walks of life with diverse experiences and backgrounds, but I connected them to God's Word. It felt impossible at first because I was just a stranger from Djibouti. I wanted to live a carefree life far from war and misery, but I never imagined to be serving God this way. The churches I established have influenced and brought people together. People who have never even met one another after several years cry on one another's shoulders in God's presence.

I remember one time when we had a praise and worship service in the city, and believers came from two different churches to attend the service. These two churches had previously been one church before splitting into two, and congregations that had not seen each other after many years began to cry on one another's shoulders in the presence of God. To our surprise, the elders of these churches walked up from the back of the church, holding hands, and singing, "We are in the Lord, and we are no longer divided."

At such a blessed moment, I honored God and realized that my calling was important; it inspired me to continue my work at Bethel Music Ministry to fulfill the mission and bring people together. "Blessed are the peacemakers, for they will be called children of God" (Mathew 5:9).

Today, the ministry has grown tremendously. We have a huge crew, specializing in specific fields like audio, visual, and media. Everyone stays connected through faith and love for God. They come from all parts of America but love one another just the same, forming a beautiful network.

As everything fell into place, I became a busy family man. I rarely had time for myself, but I was satisfied with it all. I didn't want to feel ungrateful for everything that I had already achieved because my past kept me humble. This career path was what God had envisioned for me, and I was, and still am, willing to fulfill it till the end.

Lydia, Emmanuel, and Sharon

Now, as I sit on a sofa talking on the phone with the Bethel group about the upcoming conference, Martha tidies up and irons the kids' clothes. I tilt my head, and my mind drifts to a far-off time ... I'm trudging through a desert, wrapped in a bundle of clothes, sweating bullets. I see a flag high in the sky, and I grin, noticing I have finally reached Djibouti. Then I am reminded of the time I hid under boxes in the back seat, holding my breath and feeling my heart nearly beating out of my chest.

All of a sudden, I shake my head and focus on the present. Sharon is sitting by the table and munching on cereal, while Emmanuel has his eyes glued to his phone, laughing at a video. Then I lock eyes with Martha, who jokingly scolds me to clean the tea stains on the table.

The love between Martha and me is like the first day. We are committed to the bonds of fate, and we adore each other more and more every day. I know that God has been faithful, gracious, and merciful beyond all measure throughout my journey. Therefore, I will continue to offer my life as a living sacrifice of worship for a grateful and humble response to God. It is a great thing to be called as a servant of the Lord for something extraordinary. According to Ephesians 1:4, we are chosen by God.

Fikru and Martha

Just like that, my past hardships vanish into thin air, and I heave a sigh. Looking at our children, I'm reminded that they are a blessing from God and an extension of the family that begins with the couple. I'm also grateful that they have accepted Jesus Christ as their Lord and Savior. They are well-educated young people who will become successful through their efforts in the future. The scars I received during my ordeal will eventually heal my family. As Martha and the children's laughter filled the living room, I smiled slightly at myself.

The Aligaz family

REFUGEE & HOPE

Special thanks!

My mother-in-law Ms. Haregewoin Yirdaw, and my daughter Lydia Aligaz

I express my sincere gratitude to my selfless and loving mother-in-law, Ms. Haregewoin Yirdaw. Thank you for raising our children and for everything you have done for our family over the years. Your dedication to teaching our children manners indeed paid off, and my wife and I are reaping the rewards. "Agiye," thank you from the bottom of my heart, and may the Lord bless you with many more years filled with good health.

With lots of love!

Finally, I want to leave you with my favorite Bible verse! It has helped me remember that God is always with me when I feel at my weakest. "So do not fear, for I am with you; do not be dismayed, for I am your God. I will strengthen you and help you; I will uphold you with my righteous right hand" (Isaiah 41:10 New International Version).

EPILOGUE

Coming from a war-torn country, I have a unique perspective when it comes to appreciating God's grace. I have seen firsthand the horrors of war and oppression, a stark reminder that we live in a fallen world and we all need a Savior. The Lord Jesus Christ is right there with the suffering people in every nation, in their midst, and He was with me even in my darkest hours when it seemed as though there was no hope.

My experience also taught me about humanity. I've seen the best and worst of my fellow man. Yes, there was brutality and injustice, but there were also remarkable people I encountered (I believe God put them in my path) who helped me with acts of mercy and sweet kindness. These people showed me that they were indeed the salt of the earth, preserving our fragile world from bitterness and decay.

Most of all, traveling halfway around the world and facing suffering and death more times than I care to remember, I also learned so many invaluable insights about myself. I found that I was much stronger than I ever thought I was, that my zeal to survive and to live as a free man was far more powerful than I had imagined. But it was not just my own self-interest that drove me and kept me going. It was my undying love for Martha, my future wife, and others whom I love that motivated me. I came to know and understand that God had a call on my life, to serve others and build up His kingdom through the life I would establish for myself and my family in America. And I thank Him quite literally every day for giving me the opportunity to keep that solemn promise I made to Him all those years ago.

ABOUT THE AUTHOR

Hailing from Ethiopia, Fikru Aligaz arrived in the United States through a resettlement program for refugees in 1980. The same year he reached the US, Mr. Aligaz received the Lord as his personal Savior in Arlington, Virginia. Subsequently, he became a founding member of the International Ethiopian Evangelical Church in Washington, DC.

Mr. Aligaz married his high school sweetheart, Martha Aligaz, in 1982. In pursuit of formal music education, the couple moved to Olathe, Kansas, where he enrolled in an undergraduate program in church music at MidAmerica Nazarene University and obtained his BA in 1990.

While he was a student at MidAmerica Nazarene University, Mr. Aligaz was instrumental in founding the Ethiopian Christian Fellowship in Olathe, Kansas, and served on the board of elders for four years. He also served as a minister of music and formed the first worship choir and provided music for Sunday services.

In the spring of 1992, Mr. Aligaz founded the Bethel Music Ministry. The supreme objective behind this ministry was to reach out primarily to the Ethiopian community in the United States, enrich the spiritual life of its members, and draw nonbelievers into His kingdom. The promising and resounding fame of the Bethel Music Ministry reached far and wide, prompting local churches all over the United States to invite Mr. Aligaz as a distinguished guest and share his valuable input. Over the next few years, Mr. Aligaz traveled extensively all over the United States to spread the joy of the Lord's praise through the magic of music. He has supported, through his soulful gospel music, the work of the annual Chicago conference, courtesy of the Ethiopian Evangelical Christian Association (EECA). He also took up the responsibility of directing the United Choir after the tremendous and blessed acclaim of the Bethel Choir. Mr. Aligaz articulated various duties in a well-balanced manner.

In August 1997, Mr. Aligaz completed his formal appointment with EECA to concentrate on the growth and development of the Bethel Music Ministry. During this time, he recorded one solo and four instrumental gospel albums, which have been able to carry his praise beyond the US to global shores.

In May 1998, in an unprecedented way, through the support and cooperation of fifteen Ethiopian Evangelical churches from twenty cities, the Bethel Music Ministry assembled the Bethel Praise and Worship Choir, comprised of thirty-six choir members.

For the past two decades, the choir has traveled twice a year to multiple cities in the US and Rome, Italy. The choir continues to serve the Lord while inspiring thousands of His followers.

As part of his incredible and exceptional journey, Mr. Aligaz returned to graduate school to study business administration thirty years after completing his BA and graduated from Pittsburg State University with a master of business administration (MBA) degree in December 2021.

Ever the loving and doting parents, Mr. and Mrs. Aligaz currently reside in Overland Park, Kansas, with their beautiful children Sharon and Emmanuel Aligaz. Their eldest daughter, Lydia Aligaz, graduated with an MBA and is presently pursuing an enriching and successful career. Sharon is a junior in college, while Emmanuel is a senior in high school.